To my boys,
Nick, Evan and Zack.
May you hold tight to your relationship
with God and be doers of His word in our world!

Special thanks to my wife Kathy for her love,
patience and kind words of encouragement.
And to Jenn Palmatier; thank you so much
for your critical editorial help
and encouragement!

Contents

Introduction

Have you ever had a gut feeling about something? Like when you know something's wrong and you try to ignore it, but it needles you until you do something about it? That's kind of how I felt about writing this book, only it wasn't really a "wrong" thing. In fact, it couldn't have felt more right!

At first, it started out as a small fire in my heart. I would be moved by a sermon or a song I'd hear and it seemed the feelings would last a bit longer than normal. Even after days later, I wouldn't forget how I felt and I couldn't shake the feeling off. I felt like God was pulling me closer for something. I would have dreams of Him showing me things or giving me a message to share. I found myself, more and more, seeing things through a Godly viewpoint. It was like I had a chip implanted in my brain that prodded me to a goal of not only seeking God, but sharing God. I began praying for understanding and direction and the answer popped up as plainly as the headlines of a newspaper.

It was a recurring phrase that I kept hearing over and over in different songs. I'd heard it in old hymns and in new Christian rock. The phrase was simplistic, yet so profound. It seemed so fundamental, yet clearly foundational to my walk with God and my relationship with others. So, one day, I decided to use this simple message as the text for my first New York State Vanity license plate. It read: "LERN2LUV".

Please believe me when I tell you that I'm not the type of guy that gets vanity plates. I never cared for them; most likely because they were usually, well, vain! I always thought that it was weird seeing a cryptic message on a car's license plate that clearly reflected something no one else would understand. To be fair, I have seen ones that make sense and actually stand for something worthwhile, but on the average, they live up to their namesake; vanity.

After I got my plates, I thought they would suffice as the proverbial bone I tossed to God as if saying; "OK, I get it now!" Only he wasn't nearly done with that theme and I was nowhere close to completing the task he had for me. No, the message he gave me to "Learn to Love" was just beginning to sink in. Having the plates only helped in keeping the idea and the journey fresh in my mind. Every time I'd see my car (and then the subsequent truck I traded it for), I'd be spiritually challenged to define what I really meant by what those plates implied.

Prior to this project, I think the longest essay I had ever

written was maybe six or seven pages. I don't actually consider myself a writer, or at least I didn't up until now. I spoke to my wife about it and shared that God was putting it on my heart to write a book. I thought she'd question me about it or comment on the amount of time and energy it would take or something; but she didn't. She simply said... "Do it!" I took that as a sign that God would provide the patience she would need. So I began. I sat down with my laptop one morning after seeing my youngest son off to school and just began to write.

I felt like an Angel of God was assigned to me to help me along because it took just a couple of days to bang out the first two chapters. The ideas were coming in faster than I could jot them down. It was exciting and scary all at the same time.

I found myself whispering to God for the first few days... "So this is really what you want me to do?" But when I think of how everything had happened up to that point; how much more plainly could He have spelled it out for me? I'm not saying that everything God asks us to do is easy to understand or execute, but one thing's for sure; He will open the doors for you when He wants something done!

The pace did slow up a bit as I allowed life to interrupt me now and again, but the weight of the task hasn't changed at all. I still feel that the messages I share in this book are timely and critical. We face a multitude of challenges these days, many of which are being handled in ungodly ways. It's time that we, as critical thinkers of our time, really weigh out all the evidence before us and hop off the proverbial fence. We need to choose a side; hopefully the side of good!

I pray this book helps turn the tide of our culture and turn the hearts of the people back to the one who created them because ***it is only in Him that we will have any real chance*** to learn to love in the best possible way. And in Him is the place we all need to be to begin once again.

Re-teaching Our Home Position

"I am careful not to confuse excellence with perfection. Excellence, I can reach for; perfection is Gods' business!"
Michael J. Fox

Every once in a while, as I scan the "feel good" section of the local newspaper, I rediscover this simple, yet very thought provoking parable. It's an old story, but one that is familiar to the heart of mankind. Perhaps you've heard it too. The story goes like this…

> One evening an old Cherokee told his grandson about a battle that goes on inside people. He said "My son, the battle is between two "wolves" inside us all. One is Evil. It is anger, envy, jealousy, sorrow, regret, greed, arrogance, self-pity, guilt, resentment, inferiority, lies, false pride, superiority and ego. The

other is Good. It is joy, peace, love, hope, serenity, humility, kindness, benevolence, empathy, generosity, truth, compassion and faith." The grandson thought about it for a minute and then asked his grandfather: "Which wolf wins?" The old Cherokee replied, "The one you feed!" *(Author unknown)*

There is a world of truth in that story. It seems so many of us live out our lives day by day, aimlessly floating on the perpetual waters of life. As we tarry along, we are too often oblivious to the undercurrents carrying us. Our lives have so many influences; family, friends, teachers, co-workers, music, television, movies, books, magazines; and the Internet! We are continually influenced and shaped by all these "things" that feed the wolves within us. We'd like to believe we're in control of our lives, but are we?

The popular Christian band "Switchfoot" came out with a song that asks a very poignant question; "This is your life, are you who you want to be?" How would you answer that? A deeper question we all need to ask ourselves is; "Am I who I'm meant to be?" If you've never asked that, ask yourself now!

For most of us, another question quickly follows: "How would I know?" Is the answer in finding our life's purpose or in our purpose in life? Can we tell by how happy we are with ourselves; or is it the measure of how happy others are with us?

If life teaches us anything it's this: in most cases the

strongest force wins. Whether it's in physical strength, mental ability, endurance or sheer will power; those most determined to win, find a way to muster all they have to make it happen. But is that the answer? Are we meant to be winners? Can we judge ourselves by the list of triumphs and losses we've experienced?

What is the "Thing" that would define us, thus validating our purpose in life? Some would argue that it's different for everyone. It seems each of us has been blessed with specific skills and desires that help to guide us down the countless avenues of our lives.

Is our value and purpose found in what we are able to do with our individual skills and abilities; or is our value measured by what motivates us to use them? Do the results we produce justify our means in life or would God care more about what we mean in our hearts and minds as we pursue enacting a result?

Plainly put; why are we here? As sub-atomically small as we are in the vastness of our seemingly endless universe; why do we think we deserve any special attention or recognition? We live our lives here on this tiny blue ball floating in the vastness of space needing and believing there is a purpose for our existence.

Our Purpose

With all the infinite possibilities in life, I believe there is one underlying foundation that defines our main purpose; we are here to love. I believe we were created by God to have a loving relationship with him and with each other. Of all the strongest forces ever documented throughout history, love is by far the greatest. When we consider examples like Mother Theresa, Florence Nightingale or Shah Jahan (the prince who built the Taj Mahal in dedication to his deceased wife), there is no comparison to the sacrifices made, the heroism shown or the riches lavished in the name of love.

Just the word "Love" itself conjures a warmth and tenderness that soothes the soul. The words "I love you" soften the heart and call forth our tears, while the words "I love you man" can crack the most protective shield and tear down the most hardened walls.

We've heard so much about love. It permeates every aspect of today's media. It resounds from the varied pulpits across America and whispers in armchair discussions we have with those we claim to love. Love is like a blanket we cling to whenever the world gets cold, and for those who can't feel its effects, the world is a frigid place to live.

So why discuss this now, in this book and in this manner? Why do I think we, as a nation, need to "learn to love?" The Old Testament prophecies of the Bible teach us that no matter how great a nation or cultural society thinks they are, they will fall if they ignore God's love and instruction.

Time after time, history has proven that evil destroys itself eventually. It has a self-defeating nature that runs counter to the natural forces of survival. As violent as some survival instincts may appear in nature, they are still instincts to promote life and not destroy it. Evil, on the other hand, seems bent on the promotion of death. The stark reality is that humanity as a whole has long been infested with this destructive force all throughout our history. And if pain and death by our own hands are any measure, we are getting ever worse as the centuries pass.

Alexis de Tocqueville, a famous French aristocrat who toured America in the early 1800's has been quoted* as saying the following regarding this beautiful nation of ours;

> "I sought for the greatness and genius of America in her commodious harbors and her ample rivers, and it was not there; in her fertile fields and boundless forests, and it was not there; in her rich mines and her vast world commerce, and it was not there; in her democratic Congress and her matchless Constitution, and it was not there. Not until I went into the churches of America and heard her pulpits flame with righteousness did I understand the secret of her genius and power. America is great because she is good, and if America ever ceases to be good, she will cease to be great."

I believe now, more than ever, our nation faces a pivotal point. There is a fork in the road and it's not just a liberal vs. conservative, or capitalism vs. socialism, or even a believer vs. atheist divide. I believe the core issue is choosing

---

* Although Tocqueville has many great quotes, the above has never been verified even after wide circulation. http://www.tocqueville.org/pitney.htm

whether we want to be a good people or a people that just like to feel good.

We face a moment of truth, much like the Cherokee grandson, where we need to choose which wolf to feed. We have lingered far too long, engulfed in self indulgence and personal entertainment, while forsaking the real purpose we were made for. There is an ever inflating imbalance between the freedoms and liberties we are enjoying, and the common sense responsibilities that keep them in check.

When selfishness is at the core of how we live, we deny ourselves the blessings we were meant to have; not just individually, but collectively. We miss the character growth we should be experiencing in such important human traits as honor, integrity, trustworthiness, mercy and compassion. These strengths are meant to be fostered, not through self-centered ideologies but through selfless acts of love and respect for all people.

As important as it is to love ourselves for who we are, we need to be reminded that "ourselves" shouldn't be the first person on the list. Positive self esteem is a good thing. Looking out for yourself is a good thing, but looking out for "number one" is not. The truth of this is evidenced in everything from the current divorce rates in America and the epidemic of teen sex, teen bullying and gang violence to corporate greed and government corruption at almost every level imaginable. Ours is a nation in such serious moral distress that we don't even benefit from the shock of wrong doing when we see it. For the most part, we are no longer surprised or emotionally moved by the missing child, corrupt politician or random shooting stories we hear daily. The sting is gone. Our hearts are callous.

We were created to love God first and foremost, and then to love one another as we love ourselves. Why does it have to be in that order? I would suggest it's because without putting God first, we never come to know what real love is, how it works in our lives to sustain us, or how crucial it is to protect and sustain humanity. We need to put God first so that we can understand the truth of love. In doing so we find out how real love is meant to be practiced and why it's so important for us to get it right.

The Standard

There are billions of people on the planet, all having their own perspective on what love is. A few may get it right and a few may get it wrong but most are probably a bit of both. Maybe it's time we take a step back and recalibrate ourselves against a proven standard.

In today's age of technology and automation, we have robotics that can reproduce a process at extremely tight specifications over and over at warp speeds, with unbelievable efficiency. If something breaks, the robotics needs to be "re-taught". This is a term used to describe the very refined calibration back to a known standard position that, if started from, is guaranteed to recreate the specifications and efficiencies it was built for.

For anyone confessing belief in God, he is that standard.

His will and his love is that very refined position we need to start from and recalibrate our hearts to. Our belief in God is, at its core, a submission to this truth. The more we seek him, the more we find his love to be absolutely authentic and something to strive for. As our spiritual lives mature in this truth, we learn to emulate his love in our lives as we share it with those around us.

For those who don't believe in the existence of God, I would put forth that Jesus' teachings found in the Bible are in the very least, an excellent platform to base how we are to live our lives in a structured and secure society, where all people and even creation itself can thrive. His wisdom points us to the best formula for a world of sustainable peace. But to attain the level of peace and harmony that Jesus promoted, we need to learn, and apply his understanding of love. As well intentioned as we are with our affections, we too often express love imperfectly and, at times, in a detrimental way.

We have never known a world without war and pain and suffering. We've never extinguished the fires of poverty, hunger or thirst. It should be obvious to any thinking person that the human race is in a fallen state. It's undeniable! The earth is soaked with the blood of the innocents. The corruptive power of selfishness has given ample fuel to the fires of evil that destructively sweep through our lives. As each generation passes, our world struggles more and more against the poisons we pollute it with. The sin of man has condemned us and all of creation along with it.

I believe that at the core of all our problems is a

conspicuous absence of real love the way God intended. We are somehow missing the inner compass that was meant to guide our morality, and our morality is the driving force behind the love we practice. We love because we know it's the good and right thing to do. It's instinctively ingrained into our spirits. But ever since the Fall of Man, we've been drifting farther and farther from our true mark. And the farther we drift into the darkness, the more accustomed to the dark environment we become. From there our selfish pride takes us forward and refuses to allow us to turn and look back at what we've become in comparison to what we were meant to be.

Think of all the examples we see with our own eyes; the sex, violence, corruption, greed, malice and the worst of worst, apathy. If Selfishness is our mentor, then Indifference is our brother. We cannot say we don't see it; but our inaction screams that we don't care. The truth is, in today's liberal culture, we actually seek these horrible human traits out for our own twisted entertainment. Of all the dirty and offensive words we hear every day, the one that we seem to hate most of all is CENSORSHIP!

I certainly understand the concern we have with censorship. Like most people, I would have a problem with other people telling me and my family what we can and can't read, watch or listen to. Censorship is a very slippery slope for a free government or society to go down. But the fix isn't as much in blanket censorship as it is in increasing our respect and responsibility levels to match the level of liberty that we've claimed for ourselves as "God-given" rights.

When we analyze God's plan for our lives, there is no denying that our freedom is his objective; freedom from insecurity, freedom from judgment, freedom to love and best of all, free access to him. But there are at least two things in play that limit God's ability to fulfill this objective.

The first is our lack of respect for his law, or more to the point, his will. Although there are certainly things we don't understand about God, for the most part we have a good understanding of what is right and what is wrong. All too often we choose wrong because it serves us better then doing what's right. We lie, we cheat, we steal, we deny honor to the honorable and instead worship those who entertain us. We've traded our "ownership of responsibility" card for the "but I'm a victim" card of blaming others for our sinfulness. We indulge in unholy things while we rationalize our lifestyles with patronizing laws that provide the appearance of righteousness. Over the years we have muddied the clear waters of truth so that our guilt is unseen and our children are deceived into thinking that truth is relative. We have surrounded our moral compass with self centered magnets that skew our true north and lead our children away from the high ground they were meant to be raised on.

The second real block to the freedom God plans for us lies in the fact that he is a Holy God. He can, and will love us forever, but he is forever blocked from accepting anything less than pure holiness and righteousness. The original intent for creation and mankind was a close, holy and abiding relationship with him. We broke that when we chose to walk away from him. Every day we spend with our backs to him is another day we spend in a bondage that looks deceptively like freedom.

God's answer to this problem is Jesus. Jesus came so that we could be reconciled to God even though we are a profane people. As amazingly unbelievable, wonderful and gracious that this God given, sacrificial gift is; all he asks from us is to simply turn ourselves around, look back at him and believe in this gift. That's all we need to do to save ourselves. It's really that simple!

So that I don't miss this opportunity to explain this better; allow me to lay it out for you;

- **Fact:** Jesus was a real human being that was born into the world roughly 2042 years ago. He was crucified as a heretic roughly 2009 years ago.
- **Fact:** Jesus claimed to be the Son of God. He displayed uncommon wisdom and miraculously healed people.
- **Fact:** Many people (as many as 500 or more) claimed to have seen Jesus alive after the third day that he was confirmed dead by Roman soldiers who made their living killing people.
- **Fact:** Jesus said that all we need to do to have eternal life is to believe that, because of God's love for us, his dying on the cross should be counted as the payment for our sins.

John 3:16
"For God so loved the world that he gave his one and only Son, that whoever believes in him shall not perish but have eternal life.

So all you need to do at this point is ask yourself these two questions: First, *did Jesus believe that he died to cover your sins?* The answer is yes, he certainly did. Second, *if Jesus truly believed that his death covered your sins and you can believe that he believed that, then how hard is it to take that one last step and give him the credit for it?*

If you saw a mother push her child out of the road, only to be hit by the oncoming truck herself, would you not say she died for her child? If a soldier dives on a grenade to buffer the explosion, thus saving his platoon, would he not deserve the honor of acknowledging his sacrifice to save their lives?

Jesus pushed us off the road to destruction. He dove onto the grenade meant to blow us apart. Believing that is the easy part. It's the why that stumps us! Why would a man voluntarily die for all other people? The answer is found in the first six words of John 3:16; "For God so loved the world" is why. If you believe in God, believe in Jesus' self sacrificing act. If you struggle to believe that God exists, make every effort to overcome that struggle, because there <u>IS</u> a purpose for your life! And the purpose isn't just to get by in this life dodging oncoming trucks and bombs. You are meant to love and be loved.

We have absolutely nothing to lose and everything to gain by giving Jesus credit by believing that he died for our sins. That is an essential place to start! Lest I make it sound like it stops there, I need to warn you that as the truth of that sinks in, your conscience will be moved to respond to such love. You will feel something that our culture today tends to diminish quite a bit, because it cramps our comfort level. It's the feeling of being "responsible." As you realize the magnitude of the debt that was paid, you will feel a responsibility to make the most of this gift, and a genuine yearning to get closer to the giver.

It is through this very specific acceptance of responsibility that we find true freedom the way God intended. You've heard it said, "Great freedom brings great responsibility!" The truth of this works both ways when we seek God. There is no greater freedom gained than when we take up our cross (aka. our responsibility) and follow him.

We need to begin to teach ourselves and our children the value of balancing all the freedom we enjoy with a sound ownership of moral responsibility. It's time to stop pointing fingers at others and start setting examples of goodness in our own lives. Will it be difficult? At first it will. Bad habits and addictions are hard to break. We'll need to support each other if we're going to have a chance. But we CAN do this!

Together we can help ourselves, those we love, our nation, and all of humanity if we take the time and learn to love the way God designed us to. The knowledge is already planted deep into our hearts and minds and we can bring it out if only we commit ourselves to seeking it. We need to stop denying our connection with God and allow it to once again take a rightful place in our priorities.

God can help us, and he wants to help us. We may think we know what we're doing, but without his guidance we will forever fall short. It's time we recalibrate our hearts back to his perfect standard of love.

Let's take the time and give priority to this life sustaining gift. Let today be the day that, above all things, you commit yourself to the very purpose you were created for. Using him as our music and our guide, let's once again begin the beautiful dance we were meant to share with him, and with each other. Let's rediscover the ultimate value within us all, as we seek the truth and learn to love.

Love Is............?

"We are all pencils in the hand of a writing God, who is sending love letters to the world."
Mother Theresa

I suffered divorce. Anyone who's been through a divorce can relate to the term "suffered." Besides death of a loved one, divorce has to be one of the most emotionally painful human experiences imaginable. For me, the lowest point in my life was the day that I hurt so much that I made the choice to stop loving my wife.

We met in High School and "fell in love." At least for all intents and purposes, we loved each other the way we understood love to be. The marriage lasted twenty years, which is longer then the average marriages of today and something I took great pride in. The relationship before that was on and off for five years. We had a lot of good times and bad times.

We saw sickness and health, riches and poverty, and had our fair share of laughter and tears.

Before we got married, we talked about things and decided to try living together. We each had a lot of baggage to deal with all throughout our teen years, which wreaked havoc in our relationship. We were originally engaged to be married shortly after High School, but I decided to call it off at the last minute (relatively speaking). I moved to Colorado with a friend after that so that I could have a fresh start. She stayed in New York, closer to her family, and we each gave ourselves a chance to live without the other for a while.

After about a six month separation, I realized that I still cared a great deal for this girl and decided to try and reconnect with her. We talked about our options and through the discussions, agreed that our family situations in New York seemed to be a big part of our relational problems; we thought that maybe, if we got away from there it could work. I asked her to come live with me in Colorado and before I knew it, I was back in New York to help her pack her things and move her across the country to be with me. But a funny thing happened one snowy morning while I was back east that week. I had a crisis of commitment. Not the kind you may be thinking of, though. Let me explain.

Commitment

I knew that I could love this girl for the rest of my life. I believed she was sincere when she pledged to me the same.

What I didn't have confidence in was that, without any real commitment, neither of us would give 100% to the relationship.

A lot of people think that it's better to live together rather then get married, just in case it doesn't work out. In today's American culture of divorce, I can see why people would think that. Marriage is a huge obligation and certainly not to be taken lightly. Still, when people live together, they always know that no matter what they may say, they can always walk away from the relationship if it doesn't work.

On the other hand, divorce, for as easy as it is to get these days, causes much bigger fallout. That's because marriage carries a level of honor and integrity that living together doesn't. When those are broken, there is a death attached that no amount of mourning can extinguish. Some say it's like a death that never dies. I would agree.

One of the biggest reasons for calling off the first engagement was that, the closer we got to the wedding date, the "bitchier" my fiancé got. That scared me! She always had a disgruntled edge to her that seemed manageable, but was I about to sign on to a life of nagging and yelling? Yet, here I lay, next to that same girl six months later, still looking for a promise, a real promise; a promise of love. If we were going to have any chance at this, I knew that we needed to be ALL IN! So on that snowy morning I asked her again... "Marry me?"

That one act of total commitment changed the whole dynamic of the relationship. Where fear fueled her edginess, now security and confidence fostered her tenderness. Her doubt-filled demeanor disappeared, covered over by an unstressed blanket of trust. Her held out faith in me was validated and the success of our relationship seemed secure, now more then ever. This emotional relief was shared not only by us, but by our parents and brothers and sisters as well. Everyone involved had a sense of total commitment now.

In addition to the commitment concern I had, I also had a conscience problem that the plan for living together created. I had a deep respect for my fiancé's father. He was a good man who, despite some serious challenges in his life, made the best of things and worked very hard to provide for his family. I took seriously the commandment to honor my mother and father and at that point in my life, he was a very prominent father figure to me. I knew that he didn't approve of us living together and he had very understandable concerns for the position I was placing his one and only daughter in. Yet he respected us both enough to allow us to manage our own lives. I couldn't help but feel the lack of respect I was giving him, by asking his daughter to come live with me so far away from him and the rest of her family. He deserved better then that and I thank God to this day that I made the decision to give him the respect he deserved.

Getting married was the point where perceived love displayed through the warm fuzzy feelings in our hearts was converted to the very real love displayed in action, apart from feeling. With the spiritual bond of marriage, we practiced a life of being there for each other at a much deeper, more committed level. We were fully determined to make the relationship work and so, before God and family, we tied the knot! Unfortunately for us, getting married in a church was, at that point in our lives, the only act we did that brought God into the relationship.

During our teen years and throughout the first ten years of our marriage, neither of us really took our faith seriously. I have to admit that if I had the level of faith then that I have now; I may not have gotten married (and would certainly not have lived together). Not because I wouldn't have feelings for her, but because I would have had a much better understanding of what love really costs. To commit to love is a serious sacrifice. Is it worth it? Absolutely! Just make sure that you're motives are fully understood. Too often we jump into relationships because we want to fill a hole that only God can fill. And until he is in your heart, everything coming out is at risk of being untrue.

Looking back, I can say that she loved me on her own terms and I loved her on her terms too. That's not how it's supposed to work. To be fair, had she loved me on my terms at that point in my life, it still wouldn't be right. Neither of us really understood love the way we needed to. Even worse, we didn't really know that we didn't understand. This was due to the fact that we forgot to keep God in the marriage.

His absence eventually led to our disintegration. I will never regret the decision to get married over living together and our marriage produced three of the finest human beings

I am privileged to know, namely, our sons Nicholas, Evan, and Zachary. I will, however, always regret not putting God first in my life and making him the real head of our household until it was too late.

True Definition

So many relationships are messed up today because we each have our own terms and conditions for the love we give. Right now the defensive side of you may be asking, half out loud, "What's wrong with conditions?" After all, anyone foolish enough to get into a relationship without some type of guidelines for what they expect, what they're willing to tolerate, and what they think they can bring into the relationship deserves whatever they end up with, right? I agree! Before we get ourselves knee deep in the hoopla, we should know what we're getting into and how to handle it. There's nothing wrong with expectations.

The thing I ask you to consider is; exactly where do we get our expectations from? What do we think we deserve and why? What should everyone getting into a relationship be expected to bring to it? It may sound cold to precondition our relationships with such questions, but isn't it prudent? Could we not save a lot of time, money and pain by knowing some of these things before we get involved?

If you had to write it down on a piece of paper and give it to a loved one, how would you answer that question of where you got your expectations from? Who taught you how to love? Who taught them? Where did we all get our many opinions on how to love each other? And are we right?

Anyone who's attended a Christian wedding ceremony has most likely heard the Bible's clear cut definition of love, found in First Corinthians, chapter 13, verses 4-8. In this short but concise definition, love is broken down into a simple list of "is" and "is not's". Paul writes to his friends in Corinth not about an abstract idea, but about very practical life applications. His words are about action. Allow me to take some writer's privilege and show you how I interpret what Paul is trying to convey.

Beginning at verse 4, this is how I understand it. Love is when you are being patient with others, not as an act of tolerance, but more as a practice of allowing others to learn and grow at their own pace. Love is when you do any act of kindness. Random is nice, but deliberate is more loving. Love happens every time you see something someone has and you're happy for them instead of being sad for yourself that you don't have it. Love happens when you deny yourself the bragging rights you deserve for your accomplishments, not because you have the will power to refrain from it but because in your heart you don't feel the false pride that would cause boasting to spew out of your mouth. Love is realized whenever you take care not to offend someone by your actions or spoken word, always respectfully considering the possibility of where others have been in life and what their cultural background may deem acceptable or unacceptable.

Before I continue I'd like to share a thought with you

that I have regarding a common thread found in patience, kindness, material contentment, humility and the common courtesy of respect for others. The thread I find in all of these noble traits is a deliberate removal of judgment from the heart of the wise. When we make it a point not to be judgmental of others, we find that it is much easier to love them. We need to always remember that, in most cases, we haven't walked in anyone's shoes but our own and thus we have no right to judge them. We too struggle, and need the patience, kindness, understanding and the respect of others.

This next one is very important! Love occurs naturally when we are at least as concerned for others as we are for ourselves; not just in a sentimental way but in actually meeting their needs. When your body shivers as you walk by a homeless person sleeping on the street, that's God prodding you to act. Go home and take all those old coats you have hanging in your closet and bring them to a shelter. Or better yet, return to the spot where you found someone homeless and give a coat to that person. If you get hunger pains when seeing starving people, that's God nudging you to share. Support your local Food Bank or Soup Kitchen. When you do what you can to meet these very real needs, you are sharing the love of God.

Always remember what Hebrews 13:2 says;

> "Do not forget to entertain strangers, for by so doing some people have entertained angels without knowing it."

God tests our faith and obedience through such opportunities as these we see every day. Take courage and act; by doing so you truly love your neighbor as yourself.

When you care more about the other person in an argument, you are much less likely to get angry and more able to control any anger that wells up. When you love others as much as you love yourself, it's much easier to forget the wrongs they have done to you, so that you can forgive. Forgiveness itself is a beautiful act of love and will most always bless you more then the ones you forgive. When you are disgusted by evil and injustice, and seek only truth as best you can understand it, refraining from falsehood and corruption, you practice love.

Whenever you work not to judge but to protect others, trust others, hope in their success and see these character traits through to the end, you practice love. And at the end of your life, whenever that is, if those you leave behind can say you were always there for others when they needed you, never failing to put their needs before yours, you surely have lived a life of practiced love.

The word "love" is a verb. Love is not a delicate feeling but a deliberate action. We may fall into a strong attraction for someone but with true love, we don't fall, we decide and then we act on our decision. To love someone is a choice we make, and every day we need to make it again.

Marriage is a commitment to keep making that decision every day until death separates us from physically making it anymore; at which point we cling to the feeling we had when we could. In some cases, we continue to love a person who has passed away through the act of loving others for them. Jesus showed us this example when he told his mother from the cross, "Mother, behold your son" and to John, "son, behold your mother". From that very moment on, John adopted Mary as his own mother and she did likewise to him as a son.

A Practice

A key aspect of Gods' love is that it's unconditional. It's an unfathomable concept because of our selfish nature, but there is more than enough evidence for us to have faith in its truth (as clearly demonstrated through the willing crucifixion of his one and only Son). Unconditional love is the practice of love for love's sake, apart from how it makes us feel. It's the kind of love God wants us to have for each other. He wants us to love one another, not so that we get any kind of reward but because it's the good and right thing to do.

Don't get me wrong, we are always rewarded when we love others, especially when we don't get anything back. God blesses us abundantly when we love with a selfless motive. Anyone can love someone who will return the love, thus fulfilling an expectation. That's easy! It's another story to love an ailing elderly person or sickly or troubled child or worse yet, a nasty neighbor. Yet God's simple command was to love one another; no special conditions, no strings attached, no exceptions.

God bless all the wonderful care givers of the world who are constantly sharing His love with those they care for; not because it's a high paying job (because it certainly isn't) but because they are doing God's will, whether they know it or not. When my boys were in Scouts, the troop would visit a couple of local Nursing Homes during the Christmas season where they would sing carols and hand out homemade Christmas cards. Until I participated in those visits, I really had no idea of the amount of physical and emotional support the elderly need from us. I couldn't help walking away from that experience thinking that visiting a Nursing Home would be one of the most beneficial field trips a school could take.

Love is a practice, and like all high yielding practices, love takes time to study and understand. Yet unlike high paying practices such as law, medicine or finance, we don't need a college degree to do it. It is our God given right and duty to practice love. The best part is that God himself has provided a way for us to learn. His wisdom is the curriculum and his spirit imparts the instruction. The easiest way to learn is in simply listening to God and allowing his spirit to lead.

To begin your practice, you won't need any paper or pencils, textbooks or a computer. You won't need a license or a certificate to hang on the wall before beginning, but you do need to remember that practice makes perfect. You will need to have two important tools with you at all times; you'll need an open mind and a humble heart. The world is both your classroom and your office. Allow God to lead your practice, and you will begin to see how perfect his plan really is.

The Core

Every worthy project or cause has a foundation that all other participating aspects build upon. When you dig deep, you will find a core that is indivisible and crucial to the success and true worth of what is being created. For love, God is that foundation. His nature is the full and perfect expression of selfless caring for all of us and all of creation. His son Jesus, the Christ, is the human embodiment of that nature. And for us; for our purpose to be realized, God's Holy Spirit is given to re-teach and calibrate our hearts so that we may, as best as we humanly can, practice the art of love.

God is the founder of life and master of love. It is from him that our direction and expectations need to be drawn. His love for us is that indivisible core that we're to base all we know and all we practice on. We need to get back to that. We also need to help each other remember these fundamental tenets of how we are to treat each other in life and in the loving relationships we practice. Even for people who don't believe in God's existence, his definition of love is indisputable. There is no better way. There is no deeper truth.

Sports have rules and careers have laws and guidelines. As cultures evolve, these rules and guidelines adapt. However, love isn't a game or a career. Love is foundational to life itself. It is the reason we exist, giving meaning and value to each and every one of us. For humanity to thrive, we desperately need to get this right.

The world is in distress. When we examine the facts, we have more than enough natural resources to eliminate poverty yet we still can't seem to make it happen. Wars are in constant motion due to the fact that too many people want to use their own diluted version of love and value, rather than God's. The strong oppress the weak out of selfishness and greed, and the orphan and widow are brutalized casualties. Survival of the fittest overshadows compassion and real purpose for humanity. As long as we see everything as relative, we will never find absolute peace. We can't.

God is patient and kind. He's not jealous, prideful or rude. He doesn't demand his own way. He's forgiving and not easily angered. He hates injustice and rejoices in truth. He never gives up, never loses faith, always hopes and has the power to carry us though every circumstance. Isn't it time that humanity starts loving each other like that?

Through the Lens of God

"But when anyone turns to the Lord,
the veil is taken away."
Paul the Apostle

Anyone who has ever been stuck in traffic can relate to a "bottleneck". A bottleneck is that place in the road where three lanes of traffic have to funnel down to barely one lane where you have a flagman there to make sure you're going slowly. What normally takes thirty seconds to traverse now takes fifty minutes. We hate when that happens!

In the manufacturing realm, a bottleneck means the same thing. Successful manufacturing is all about "thru-put", a term given to the amount of product a specific step in the process can produce. If you can attach four wheels to a toy fire truck at the rate of seventy trucks an hour, but you can only attach ladders to forty trucks in that same hour, then attaching the ladders part of the process is your bottleneck.

Bottlenecks are the manufacturer's nemesis. If they can figure a way to improve the thru-put of the slowest step in the process, they can increase the overall thru-put of their manufacturing line. And more thru-put means more profits for the business.

As you can imagine, some steps are, by design, a bottleneck. In the process of making microchips, the Lithography process is such a step. Litho, as it's called, is a natural bottleneck for two main reasons. The first is cost. Lithography tools are typically only ten percent of the tooling but account for as much as twenty five percent of the manufacturing budget. Plainly put, it's the most expensive part of the process.

The second reason Litho is a bottleneck is that it's the step in the process with the hardest technological challenge. The microchip race is all about shrinking the devices so that you can fit more on a chip. Where we used to make hundreds or thousands of transistors on a microchip, we now make millions and billions. How can we put so many more devices on the same little piece of silicon real estate? The answer is in the Lithography. The more sophisticated the lens and associated alignment package, the smaller and cleaner the image printed. Some state of the art lenses used today are worth over a million dollars each.

Anyone really into photography knows that a good lens makes all the difference. With a high quality lens that is customized for a specific type of shot, the pictures are more clear, more colorful, more vibrant and detailed. One magazine that provides world class photography is National Geographic. The world as viewed through the eyes of their photo staff is nothing short of awe inspiring. It is amazing what they can do with a camera, and I'd bet that a crucial part of that is because they use only the best lenses.

So as not to stray too far from the point, I should get back to the bottleneck concept, specific to Lithography. Since it's both the most expensive step and the hardest process to master in making microchips, I think it's fair to say that it's a very critical step in the overall microchip making process.

Focus

What does all this have to do with love? I'm glad you asked! If learning to love is a process; one that, for some, seems to be as difficult as making microchips, then God is the bottleneck! God is like that critical step that throttles the process and, depending on how we utilize him, controls the ultimate success that our lives produce. And like Lithography, the outcome depends on what we do with the lens of God.

A lens has three main functions. I'll cover the first two as they relate to focus and the last I will get to later in the chapter. The first function I'd like to explain is how a lens is used to bring something into a precise focal plane.

Everything you see with the naked eye is in a specific focal plane. Try a simple exercise. Hold out your pointer finger and look at it. While you are looking at it, without taking your eyes off of it, see how well things behind it are in focus for you. Chances are they will be a bit blurry. That's because they are on a different focal plane. Our eyes naturally do the math and balance multiple focal planes in view so we generally see many things clearly at different distances at once. However, if you really try to look precisely at one thing, the things in front and in back of it get a touch out of focus.

The second function of a lens is just the opposite of the first. In photography, there are some things you don't want to print and a lens can be precise enough to actually remove anything from a picture that is outside the exact distance you are focusing on. The next time you get the chance to look into a microscope, watch as you turn the dial. You'll see things come and go from view. What you are doing is drifting from one acute focal plane to the next.

In Lithography, a reproducible image is etched into a chrome film on a glass plate. These plates are used as template masks to print specific patterns onto planarized (extremely flat) silicon wafers. Much like an ordinary camera, light is flashed through the mask and the patterned image is transferred to a photo resist layer applied to the wafer, leaving a picture of the image desired after developing. At tolerances as tight as they need to manufacture today's leading edge microchips, the smallest particle of dirt or dust could ruin the image. To solve this problem, each glass plate is equipped with a pellicle. A pellicle is a very thin sheet of cellophane mounted to a raised ring around the etched image.

This clear thin sheet actually protects the image by changing the focal plane of any dust or dirt that may land over it, so when the image is shot, these particles don't print.

So to recap, we've covered two functions of a lens. The first is to refine what you want coming through and the second is to filter out what you don't want coming through. Here's where God comes in. No matter how hard we try on our own to print an acceptable picture of love, we as humans fail to provide what was originally intended. If you compare us to one another, many of us aren't bad at all. We love in ways that make us and our mothers proud! But when we compare it to the standard that we were created to use, we fall miserably short.

When we invite God into our heart it's like placing a highly calibrated, extremely polished and refined lens in front of the love that comes out of our souls. Only God's spirit can bring our hearts into such focus that we are able to clearly recognize and practice the real love we were meant to share. At the same time, he removes some of the worldly influences that degrade our love; helping our hearts to recognize them for the useless dirt and dust they are. He changes our focus away from detrimental things of this world and realigns it to things that support physical and spiritual health.

In our current state, we have dirty filters that block and blur our understanding of love, and we are incapable of loving others as we were made to. Only through the lens of God can we reach the refined potential we were originally designed to live and love at. And only with his lens can we see how far out of focus our current state of being human is.

Clarity

Before I invited God into my heart I considered myself to be a nice guy. I was a good husband, a good father and respectful of my elders; but I was also a man who enjoyed looking at girls. I never cheated on my wife but I didn't see a problem with dirty magazines or movies. I didn't frequent strip clubs at all, but one day I was invited to join a bachelor party at a local club with some of my old high school friends.

It happens that at the same time in my life I was struggling with the state of my spiritual health. In my youngest days I was raised Catholic and then through a series of events my family fell away from that faith. My father had also struggled with his spiritual health and through my early teen years we studied various Eastern religions together. We eventually returned to a Christian faith and I half heartedly confessed belief in it, not because I didn't believe it was true (although I did have a lot of questions), but because I wasn't ready to do what God was asking.

On the day I was supposed to go to the bachelor party, I was sitting at a spiritual crossroads. I had bought a tattered Good News Bible from a used book store which, ironically enough was located across from the strip club. I had recently found a Christian radio station and had that dialed in. A very timely song was playing; Michael W. Smith's "My place in this world". As I read the Gospel I decided to finally take a stand. With the most genuine humility I had ever felt, I prayed; "God, if you're there, I need to know. I need a real sign from you. I want to believe but haven't seen anything yet to believe in. Help me to see you. Please open my eyes and come into my heart. I want to love you but I don't know how. Please show me."

By the time I was done, I was weeping. I felt humiliated but I also felt more peace then I had felt in years. I realized that I had, for the first time in my life, really committed to live for God more then for myself. But I was still in the world wasn't I? I was still a husband, father and friend who promised he'd be at the bachelor party. So I went in. But I was different.

For the first time in my life I saw these beautiful girls with a God-like clarity. They were no longer strippers or objects of entertainment; they were real people like me. I didn't see a strip tease, I saw my sister. She wasn't just a play thing, she was someone's daughter. She didn't seem to know it but I did. Needless to say it was a rather short visit for me. I had a fist full of dollars I had gotten ahead of time, but things had drastically changed. As others swaggered up with lewd movements, tenderly sliding dollar bills into provocative spots, I could only walk straight up with tears in my eyes, place the dollars in her hand and hug her like she was my kid sister. I whispered in her ear that God loved her more then anyone here. I must have scared her because she backed up and shot me this look as if I was the craziest person on the planet.

I turned and walked away and before I knew it, I was back out in my car. At that point I restarted my conversation with God, only this time I was overjoyed and extremely thankful. God had given me a sign. He had shown me in a tangible way how very real he is, and what life can be like when he's living inside me.

For the first time I actually experienced life as seen through the lens of God. The shallow, materialistic, self centered veil was lifted from my face and I could see the reality of sin and the conquering power of real love over it, exposing it for what it is. Before that moment, my view of life was out of focus. Love to my understanding was a feeling I had for people, mostly. But feelings can deceive! Sin is often camouflaged under the guise of feeling good.

God showed me in the middle of a bachelor party that love isn't about feeling. In that instant, love was about allowing me to see this human being as he sees her and inspiring me to go up and meet her financial need while telling her about him. My feeling bad for that girl wasn't enough. For me to really love her as I loved myself, I needed to act.

That experience was life changing for me. I wasn't made perfect then and I'm not perfect now, but what I did right was this; I put God first! I fell away in humility and allowed him to drive my heart and mind. I allowed God to slip his perfect lens in front of my hearts' eyes so that I could see life from his perspective, driven by his purpose. It was as if God had removed from my eyes, rose colored glasses I didn't even know I was wearing. The scary thing is that I would have never known I had those mind fogging, vision blurring and conscience dulling glasses on, had I not taken that simple leap of faith.

Maybe it was all those prayers my Mom said for me over the years. Or maybe it was my Father's intense search for the truth and his insatiable curiosity of spiritual matters. Maybe it was all those people in my life that God had used, one way or another to nudge me to the decision to once again seek His word in that raggedy old Bible I spent all of three dollars on. Whatever it was, it worked.

I'm sure there'll be many a decision I'll regret making in my life by the time I'm done, but I can say without a doubt that on that day, in my car, I made the best decision of my life. You've heard it said that ignorance is bliss. What you may not have heard is that ignorance can kill. It's funny how sometimes we don't even know we're in trouble until it's too late. If only we would have known.

I realize that in today's culture it's hard to trust anyone or anything. Family lets us down. Our friends let us down. The government.......well, you get the point! We want control because control feels safer than trust. When we do trust it seems that we aren't paying enough attention to who we're trusting in. We are taught that pain is always bad and comfort is always good and we should strive to get what we can because no one's going to hand it to us. It's OK to help others, just make sure you help yourself first. But what if all that is backwards?

When you put God first in your life you'll be amazed at how differently you view the world and the people in it. God's version of love lifts us above the clouded views of religion, politics and economics. It clears the smoke of indifference and neutralizes the sting of fear. Like a finely crafted lens it helps our hearts focus in on the important things of life, while removing nonsense from our view. We not only see people's needs more clearly, but we feel the weight of them more as well. We see sin more acutely and start to understand how pervasively it's grafted itself into our lives. We also gain a better vision of the actions we should be taking to share God's love in a broken world.

Magnifying the Power

I promised I'd share the third function of a lens with you. It's the one most people are familiar with (just ask the crazy little kids outside with a magnifying glass looking for bugs to fry!). The third function of a lens is magnification. A lens has the power to make something very small, even invisible to the naked eye, look bigger than life. But wait, there's more because as they say, "looks aren't everything". Not only can a lens make something look bigger but in the case of the crazy kids looking for bugs, a lens can actually increase the intensity of a given force; in their case it would be the sun's heat.

The process is simple enough. The sunlight hits the glass on the top and the shape of the glass bends the light to the middle so that all the energy comes out the bottom in a concentrated way. Another way to look at it is that it takes something very scattered and random and organizes it, giving it specific direction to be highly efficient and much more powerful. It seems simple but it's actually pretty amazing!

Now, imagine that your heart emits a constant light. That light in turn carries on its beam all the love that you generate. Some people go through life naturally bright. They just seem to emanate enthusiasm and good feelings wherever they go. However, some people, on the other hand, for whatever reason, seem to be low light emitters. They are content to keep to themselves, rarely looking up as they walk by you and even more rarely smiling. The one thing we all have in common, whether we're beaming or struggling, is that we can all do better. Whenever we try on our own, without direction, we are always less efficient then someone who gets the professional help and tools they need to do the job right.

Wouldn't it be great if someone invented a magnifying lens that we could slip in front of our hearts, which would automatically fine tune and multiply the light coming out of our lives? Even the smallest amount would light up a room! And what if at the same time the magnifying lens helped our eyes to see truth more clearly so that what we think is good is really good and what we see as bad is so obvious that we'd all be helping each other stay clear of it? And what if this lens also had a continuous calibration feature that re-taught the heart and mind on a regular basis so that the individual would always be improving in strength and integrity?

There is an optimum state of being human. There is a best case scenario for our nation and humanity. When we put ourselves first, we win sometimes and lose sometimes. When we put others first we win sometimes and lose sometimes. But if we all put God first, others second and ourselves last, think of the possibilities we'd have. Instead of truth being relative to whoever's point of view, we'd all agree on what truth is. Instead of giving what we can on our own we'd be able to give so much more and in turn, receive so much more back.

From a human perspective, I admit I don't understand some of God's rules but I do know they are for the good of us all. When I put him first, what I want isn't as important. With God directing my life, I find it impossible to hate people for thinking differently then I do. I don't agree with a lot of what's going on in our nation or in the world today but I believe most of it is based on people putting themselves first. We want what we want and we're willing to ignore the pain it causes others to get it. For humanity to be blessed at the level we were meant to be, this has to stop!

We need to be re-taught! We need to be tuned and calibrated. We need to be filtered to protect us from sin's contamination. We need someone to remove the "blur" colored glasses we don't even know we're wearing. We desperately need to see the world through the beautiful lens of God!

Only God can get us back to the standard; the known good position that we were created to start from. As good as we think we may be, we're no where close to the greatness that God has in store for us if we'd only put him first and let him lead in every aspect of our lives. Before we move any further away, let's allow God to bring us back to that position behind his lens where our true beauty and greatness begins.

Religion vs. Relationship

"A journey of a thousand miles begins with a single step."
Confucius

I was asked to cover for my pastor one Sunday since he'd be out of town. I didn't have to do the whole service; he just needed me to do the sermon. As always, I was humbled, honored and excited for the chance to speak for God. It just so happened that I had been reading a book entitled "Heaven" written by Randy Alcorn at the time. It's an excellent book that answers many a question you may have about this place we all hope to go to after we're done here. I found the book's theme to be very inspiring and decided that I would use the opportunity to share that inspiration with the congregation.

The great thing about doing sermons is that I learn far more than I teach to others. On the path of preparation

I find so many important facts I really need to move my faith forward. Had I not accepted the privilege of doing the sermon, I would have missed them completely. I challenge anyone serious about their faith to actually write a sermon. It takes you quite a bit deeper than a normal bible study and in the spirit of learning to love, it is very eye opening. It's one thing to understand something and believe it. It's quite another to have to articulate a truth into an efficient twenty minute speech that you hope and pray fully represents God's message and purpose.

The Important Thing

The main point of the sermon was to raise the level of curiosity about Heaven in the congregation; but through it I found the exercise helped me to see some of my own misunderstandings as well. As I reviewed my personal spirituality, I realized that I wasn't thinking (or living) "long term" enough. I accepted the norm of keeping this world separated from the next; but I found that the two worlds are actually much more connected then I originally perceived.

My lead-in described all the preparations my wife Kathy and I made for a recent trip to California, to visit her brother and his family. I began with the fact that we scheduled the vacation time with our place of employment months in advance. Shortly after that, we booked the airline tickets and a car rental and began to save some spending money. As the time grew near, we began to shop for gifts for each member of their family. We brought them home, wrapped each one and then we went to the UPS store to have them shipped out ahead of us so that they'd get there the day after we arrived. (Yeah, it is a cool idea...of course it was Kathy's).

We carefully packed our things as not to exceed the weight limits at the airport. We reviewed maps of California close to where we were going and discussed various "must see" places so that we wouldn't miss anything, relatively speaking. We even pre-programmed specific addresses into our GPS so that when we got to the airport in California and made it to our rental car; we'd just select an entry and know exactly where to drive and how long it would take to get there. Finally, we notified family members of our travel details in case of emergency.

By the time we were scheduled to leave, we had put in a lot of thought and preparation for this trip we were making. So it struck me! Here I spent all this time and effort learning about and preparing for a place I'd spend a week of my life and yet when it came to Heaven, I was virtually clueless! Apart from some basic concepts and story book images, I had very little knowledge of this place I'm hoping to spend eternity in.

A good number of people came up to me after church and said they had never given Heaven much thought or ever heard of the concept of an intermediate Heaven. They assumed Heaven would be a great place but hadn't thought about it actually being this place, resurrected and restored to its original design before the curse of sin entered in, as described in Randy Alcorn's book "Heaven." They were glad for the sermon because it sparked a new curiosity in their heart for the subject of Heaven and eternity.

The funny thing is that you might assume that as Christians we would all think about Heaven a lot, but evidently we don't. I imagine it's hard to think about such a place when you know that, to get there, you have to go through a door no one really wants to open. The reality of death and all its ramifications conjures only sadness and feelings of loss for most people. It helps me to remember that as a believer, I am already living in Eternity and I trust in Gods' love enough that when I physically die, or when those I love die, our spiritual bodies will be in a much better state then they are now. From there we will remember our lives here and, as Mother Theresa once said, "All the pain and suffering we feel in this world will seem as having only to spend one night in an inconvenient hotel."

As I pondered the lack of knowledge we collectively have about our eternal destination, I began thinking about a much bigger theme. As Christians, how much studying have we done on the true definition and practical applications of love? Sure we've heard a billion songs, saw a ton of movies and heard many a love story over the days of our lives, but when it comes down to understanding it the way God explains it, can we really pass a test? More then anything else we learn here on Earth, understanding love has got to be paramount. After all, isn't love the key that will open the door to Heaven?

In chapter 10 of the book of Luke, an expert of the

Torah (God's law for the Jews) asked Jesus what he must do to acquire eternal life:

> "Teacher," he asked, "what must I do to inherit eternal life?" "What is written in the Law?" Jesus replied. "How do you read it?" The expert answered: "Love the Lord your God with all your heart and with all your soul and with all your strength and with your entire mind and, love your neighbor as yourself." To this Jesus affirmed, "You have answered correctly".

As much as we should know about the place where we hope to spend eternity, all the more we should know about exactly what God meant in these verses so that we too can inherit eternal life. My sermon probably should have been based on the importance of learning to love first, so that we can get into Heaven. In hindsight, that would be the logical order. But it appears God knows human nature well enough to know that we all need to see a prize before we will ever begin the journey to get it.

Our Passion

Just like the prophets of long ago, telling God's message to people is not always easy, especially if it goes against popular cultural views. It's easy for us to hide in seclusion with our private beliefs, separated from those who would challenge us. But once we take that step of faith and ask God to take control of our lives; once we truly begin a relationship with God, we are forced to deal with these counter cultural feelings that rise up from deep within our souls. Here is where many a believer gets themselves into trouble and, by default, put our human understanding of God into trouble as well.

Have you ever met a person that is defined by their religion, but in a bad way? Maybe it's the bible beating woman whose face turns stoic and angry whenever she hears the words "abortion" or "homosexual." She whips anger and judgment out of her back pocket and holds them up like trump cards she saves to use whenever the opportunity arises. Or maybe it's the tightly "suit and tied up" man who mumbles under his breath whenever he sees the teenage girl with the nose ring sitting two pews away. In utter disgust, he rehearses his weekly thought; "How dare she take communion looking like that!"

The problem we have sometimes with our religion is the fact that we've lost track of the relationship part. Isn't that where it all started? Wasn't that the ultimate "baby's first step" when we came to God in complete humility? Didn't we commit to his leading when we accepted his invitation to a real relationship with him, whether through a baptism, confirmation, bar mitzvah, bat mitzvah or just a simple, heartfelt prayer? Our answer to these questions, if we are truly seeking God, should be a resounding YES! After all, the relationship is what it's all about.

Even when we look at the basic concept of relationship from a scientific perspective, we clearly see how integral it is to our species. Whether you are an Evolutionist or a

Creationist, you can't argue with the fact that as we trace ourselves all the way back, we still come from one source. We are indelibly and intrinsically related to each other. No matter what we do or what belief system we ascribe to, our relationship is already established. All we are asked to do to optimize humanity, is apply God's love to that relationship.

We started with love; it's what we were created for. God is always patiently waiting for us to turn back to him and accept his love. The first and foremost thing he wants to do is teach us how to love him back, and how to love others as he does. That's not a religion thing, that's a relationship thing. That needs to be where our passion comes from; a very real and present relationship with God.

Religion is a good tool to promote disciplines that help us stay healthy and safe in life. It helps us stay focused on our priorities. Webster's Dictionary defines religion as *"scrupulous conformity"* and *"a cause, principle, or system of beliefs held to with ardor and faith."* It's a serious dedication to something. For me, that something is my relationship with my Creator.

God uses us, his created people as teaching aids and practice vessels to share his nature; we are to be conduits of His will. But to do this accurately we need to be in a relationship with him. One definition of relationship is having *"a romantic or passionate attachment."* Some say of people they know, that they are passionate about their beliefs. When it comes to God we should view it as being passionate about our relationship with him, thus we attempt to scrupulously conform to his image, as we were created to be.

We learn things by seeing, listening, copying and practicing. Anything worthwhile always takes time to get right. There are very few shortcuts in life, especially when what we're gaining really counts. Our understanding of love is something that really counts. How we practice love depends on our understanding of what it is, where it comes from, and why we have it. As we allow the Holy Spirit to guide us and teach us, our passion for God is deepened as our relationship with him is strengthened. By following Jesus, listening to his teaching and emulating his love, we build on our relationship by learning to love others as God loves us. In this we come to realize the very real and genuine relationship that all humanity shares.

Lead to Follow

We need to help each other remember that religion is but a tool to achieve the goal, which is to develop a close relationship with God. I absolutely recommend finding a place of worship that you are comfortable with; one where your faith is strengthened and your spirit nourished toward the will of God. God's word tells us that iron sharpens iron. He knows that in the practice of love, the whole is always greater than the sum of the individual parts. That said; claiming a denomination or being a member of an organized church isn't a necessity for building a relationship with God. Understanding God's will for you as explained in his word, and holding tightly to his hand every day is the necessity. Once we let go of God's hand, we risk straying off his narrow path and into the world's view of how we are to love one another. It is because too many of us follow man's word instead of God's that we are in such a condition as we are today.

The world likes to judge and condemn. It is also very accepting of ungodly things. God accepts us for who we are. He always has. He hates ungodly things in our lives, but he loves us even as we accept ungodly things. He wants to help us understand this truth and help us to do the same for each other. As we begin to understand and believe in his love and become more open to it, we begin to lose our fascination with ungodly things and become fascinated with God instead.

We should never embrace sin, but we need to always give God the ability to embrace others, by allowing his love to flow through us. We all sin, yet we all have the capacity to love despite ourselves. We need to concentrate less on what we feel is right or wrong and more on what God says is the priority, which is to love him with everything we have and love one another as ourselves. If we do that, he will be faithful to fix us.

We were created to have loving relationships. We start our relationship with God when we open our hearts to his love. To accomplish this, we have to remove ourselves from being first, and place him in that spot instead. Once we do that, he begins to teach us through his word, through people, through music, books and a whole host of things we see and hear every day. All we need to do is remember him and, as we take baby steps, allow him to lead us.

When we drift, he will always bring us back to the home base of loving first; only then can we lovingly agree to disagree with others, even if we feel they do ungodly things. The hard truth for us is that he will help us to remember the planks in our own eyes, as we point and sneer at the splinters in others. This, in turn, will help us to love in truth as he does.

As children of God, we need to remember what Paul said in Romans 3:23; that we have all sinned and fallen short of the glory of God. Every day we need to start there. I realize that some people try to redefine sin to accommodate their way of thinking and living. We will all be judged some day by God and we all need to remember that the judgment IS HIS and NOT OUR responsibility! Our responsibility is to love him and love one another. As long as we put him first, we will have the strength to do that.

God alone can show us how to meet each other's needs without compromising our values. As we turn to him for guidance on dealing with the ungodly, he teaches us what he means when he said "return Evil with Good". He didn't teach "tolerance" the way it's taught today, but he does teach that love overcomes evil without having to accept or embrace it.

The greatest tragedy we can perform is to deny anyone God's form of love or the ability to practice it. That's not what he's about. No one will ever have the right to redefine his written law and what it labels as sin, but we are all obligated to uphold the most important command ever written, which is to love him and love others. Cultures come and go, human laws get written and revoked, but the command to love always was, always is and will always be, throughout eternity. We would do much better as a species if we remember that fact!

We will never be in better hands; we will never have a better parent and friend. All great journeys start with a step. This is your chance to begin eternity today. When you stray, as we all do, there is hope. Just turn around again and reach out for the love of God and I promise you, he will bring you to the good path again. Never give up and never believe the age old lie that God couldn't possibly love you after what you've done.

If you've messed up a million times, he's forgiven you a million and one. Nothing you can ever do can neither earn, nor stop his love for you. The number one step in learning to love is keeping God first in your life so that through him, you will come to know what true love is, as you receive it from him and share it with others.

The Fact of the Matter

"..When you feel like compromising, just remember
I'll be right there smiling down on you."
Pillar

For me, the journey with God has to restart every day. They say God's grace is new every day and I have found that to be abundantly true. What I've also found is, the impact of God's grace in my life is in direct proportion to the level of my commitment to receive it daily; to do that, I need to receive Him daily.

God is a person of his word! He never breaks a promise and never denies us his love. He is always there, patiently walking with us like a parent on a nature trail trying to keep his kids out of the poison ivy! It's us who continue to leave him, if even for a short while, to do our own thing. Curiosity is a positive and acceptable nature that God gave humanity. But I think his original intention was that we be curious *with* him by our side and *not* on our own. Like all good parents, God knows all too well, the dangers that curiosity brings.

We are so distracted by the "shiny things" of this world that we can't help ourselves. Whether its sports, work, politics or even church activity, we seem to forget that we are supposed to stay in a constant relationship with God. Like the air we breathe, the bodies we have and the souls that indwell our bodies, God is to be there with us for every moment, every decision and every thought. But the thought of that fact scares us doesn't it?

For the past few years I've had the privilege of bringing some of our church teens to a summer camp in the Adirondacks of upstate New York. We participate in all the classic fun stuff like hiking, canoeing, team challenge activities and of coarse, camp outs. We also make sure we get our Daily Devos (devotions) in every morning and night.

During night time Devos, the counselors like to put on a skit that both entertains as well as provokes faith questions for the kids to discuss. One of my all time favorite skits was one that I proudly watched my son and his friends put on for the counselors and the younger kids camping out with us. The point of the skit was to get everyone (myself included) to imagine what it would be like if we could actually see God.

The Skit

It started with a boy named Zack, presumably kneeling by his bed and praying the invitational prayer to God.

Zack: *"God, I believe you're there, and I am really sorry for the mistakes I've made. I wasn't following you. Please God, come into my heart and stay with me and guide me, so that I follow your will instead of my own. Amen!"*

The boy lies down for the night and in the morning (3 seconds later), he gets up to get ready for school. He walks over to his closet to grab a shirt, and when he opens the door, God is there!

God: *"Good Morning Zack! Are we getting ready for school? Can I help?"* God says with a big smile, proud of the rekindled relationship.

But the boy is stunned!

Zack: *"What the...how did you get...wait a minute!"*

God acknowledges the boy's confusion and explains the puzzling situation.

God: *"Didn't you pray for me to come into your life and stay with you and guide you?"*

Zack: *"Well yeah, I did,"* Zack exclaims; *"but I didn't mean like...literally!"*

God reaches out and hugs him.

God: *"Too late! I'm here to stay and I'll never leave you, so don't you worry. From now on you're never alone!"*

They make their way to the breakfast table and the family is equally puzzled.

Zack's Mom: *"Zack, who's your friend?"*

Zack: *"Uhmm, this is uhmm..."* Zack stumbles out as God interrupts.

God: *"I'm God! Good morning everyone!"*

The mother quickly extinguishes her cigarette and the father stops mid sentence because the second half of what he was saying included words that rhyme with chucking spit. The boy, feeling rather uncomfortable and cornered, quickly excuses himself and runs for the door blurting a white lie about being late for school. God quickly follows and before you know it, they're on the school bus.

Friend #1: *"Who's your friend?"*

Friend #2 *"Isn't he a little old to ride the bus?"*

His friends snicker as they size up this new person in Zack's life. Embarrassed, Zack makes a quick excuse and brushes it off. Just then, one of the boys breaks out a porno magazine he snuck from his father's stash and starts showing it to his friends. Knowing full well what it is; God asks a question to make a point.

God: *"What's that? Can I see it?"*

Zack: *"NO! You don't want to see that."*...almost screaming in panic. Then God, looking straight at Zack, says....

God: *"Why not? You do!"*

God's response hangs in the air as the reality of it sinks into Zack's heart. He realizes that God was right, and because God didn't really want to see the magazine, neither should he. At this, Zack takes a defining stand with his friends.

Zack: *"Guys, this is God and I asked him to come into my life and lead me. I want to hang out with you guys but I can't hang out with that,"* pointing to the magazine. *"I'm sorry guys; I think I'd better move to a different seat."*

At that comment, the other boys look at each other and then turn their faces down in shame.

Friends #1 together: *"You're right Zack. We shouldn't be looking at stuff like this either."*

Without looking up because of their new found guilt, they ask God,

Friends #1: *"We guess you're mad at us aren't you?"*

God smiles and says…

God: *"No, I'm actually proud of you guys for doing the right thing now. Would you guys mind if I hung out with you too?"* The boys instantly light up and then, without missing a beat, break out a Motocross magazine and with excited pride say,

Friends #2: *"God check out this magazine!"*

The Moral

I appreciate this short but powerful story because it strikes at the very core of our shortcomings regarding our "real" relationship with God, and our misunderstanding of love. Love isn't something we fall into or out of. Love is something we choose to do, and do responsibly. It's a decision we make and follow with action.

A marriage is successful when both parties put the others' need before their own and keep the commitment they made; to keep loving no matter what. How many couples do you know who got divorced because they "fell out of love," or confess that they just don't love each other any more? The latter is the most accurate, but it has little to do with feeling and a lot to do with inaction on one or both parties in the relationship.

Since love is action, how would we all act (love) if God were visible to us; always present, breathing down our necks, hanging over our shoulders? We wouldn't want that, would we? Actually we would! Maybe not at first because we'd have to give up our selfishness and replace it with the burden of entertaining a very righteous and Holy God; but after a period of time, when we got to know God for who and what he is, we'd be fine. We'd be much happier, healthier and loving people then we are now. We would learn first hand how to love him and love others in a way we never imagined; God's way!

Imagine if everyone who claims to be Christian actually lived as if God was right there with them every minute of every day. We'd never again wonder "what would Jesus do" because we could ask him ourselves through heart felt, and faith filled prayer, and his mere presence would provide more than enough courage and strength to handle any temptations we'd face. Imagine how fun it would be to always have the one around that actually created laughter! Imagine the reassurance we could tap into whenever we struggled with fear and doubt, with loss or defeat.

Let's think a little bigger now. Imagine what it would be like if most all of the problems we face today simply disappeared; insecurity, inadequacy, prejudice, violence, injustice, intolerance, temptation and even many of our financial struggles. If I had to pick a "god" that everyone seems to serve and worship it would have to be money! But can we really imagine if money was never a problem for anyone anymore? (I mean like without us being dead yet!)

Imagine a man losing his job and everyone in the

community pulling together to support his needs until he finds work. Half a dozen people in his community would offer him a job knowing that, with God always around, he'll always do his best. A Grandmother addicted to scratch offs could break free from the grips of gambling and have more money each month to pay her bills. Wouldn't it be nice if everyone made a wage that truly reflected the work they put in, based on what they were doing with the skills and abilities that God gave them, and not their own inflated worth? What a refreshing change from people taking advantage of others based on what this world says they could get for their supposed services.

Imagine things always being sold at a fair price. Imagine the drop in taxes when politicians become honest and big business stops lobbying. Imagine CEO's actually looking out for the best interest of all their employees and not just VP's, Board members and themselves. Imagine a stock market that was measured by the needs it met rather then the margins it gained. Imagine no more frivolous law suits.

Imagine kids never picking on other kids. Imagine the single mom having an abundance of trustworthy people to watch her children for her and a place where she can get her car fixed without getting ripped off.

Teen pregnancy would drop dramatically and abortion would be rare and never out of convenience. Drug abuse would drop; alcoholism would drop; and domestic violence would never again ruin a family. Police officers would have to find all new ways to serve the public (although even with

God in the car, some people would still drive fast!).

The fact of the matter is that the world would be a radically different place if people who say they believe in God actually lived as though they could see him standing next to them. And if God didn't love us as much as he does, he would be more visible. But he does love us, way more than we know.

Free Will

Anyone who is a teenager, was a teenager, or is the younger sibling of a teenager knows that teenagers like their privacy and independence. To God, we're all teenagers! We know just enough to get ourselves into trouble, but we're so sure we know how to keep out of trouble that we walk right into it all the time. How many teenagers do you know that really understand the fact that they don't know even half of what life is all about yet? Yeah...me neither! We all want our independence and don't particularly enjoy hanging out with our parent(s); and because he loves us so much, he honors that request.

Free will is the gift of love and at the same time, love's most important ingredient. God gives us the *freedom* to choose whether we want to be with him or not. Any other arrangement couldn't really be a relationship based on true love. For love to be real, God had to allow us the *free will to choose* Him over ourselves. That's why he is hidden; so we have the free choice to either seek him out or ignore his existence. If you ignore him he'll honor your decision. That doesn't mean he won't continue to love you or try to get your attention but he will never force himself on anyone.

If you decide to seek him out, you will find him and you will be moved to love him because of the love you will find in him. He will make himself evident if you truly seek him with a humble heart. But it's totally your choice!

We all need our Father! As nice as privacy and independence are, they get us into trouble. The reality is that we weren't created to be so fiercely independent. We were created to be in relationships, the most important one being with our Creator.

When we, as a people, begin to see God with our hearts and lives in such a way that he is ever present, then we'll begin to radically change our nation and our world with his love! God's law is good, but God's love is better in that it fulfills the law while defining its purpose. Many of us live only by the laws that the government makes. The problem is the government isn't perfect and in some cases, it's corrupted by greed and the selfishness of our culture.

Gods' law defines and exposes our sin. But God's love can cover our sins and help us out of them and into a better place. All we need to do is start and sustain a close relationship with God. It's never been about religion. It has always been about a relationship. Can you imagine how great our communities would be if we all took that relationship seriously and lived as if God was actually physically living with us?

At camp, we do this thing at the end of the week where

we get a piece of yarn and we tie it around each others wrists to remind us of the relationships we've forged during the week. It's a tradition that has been carried on for many years. My yarn usually lasts about eight or nine months before it gets to a breaking point. But throughout that time it is a pleasant reminder of all the fun I had and lessons I had the privilege to both teach and learn! Most of all it reminds me that I'm forever in a relationship with a very loving God.

I challenge you to find a length of yarn, cut it into enough pieces so that everyone in your household can have one and then take turns tying them around each others wrists. It's not to remind you all of who's in the house but rather who you are all in a relationship with. Let it remind you every day that God is always right there, standing with you!

Where Your Treasure Is

"Give me five minutes with a person's checkbook and I'll tell you where their heart is!"
Billy Graham

When I was little, I flipped baseball cards. I could say I collected them but I'd be lying. It was much more like playing with them than collecting them. The game went that each card had a color border and you and other kids would take turns flipping them onto a pile. If I flipped a green on top of a green someone just put down, I'd win the pile!

To give you an idea of which cards I had, I was born in 1960. Mickey Mantle was considered to be one of the best cards to have. Tom Seaver was a Rookie and Don Wilson, Hank Aaron and Willie Stargell were popular in my day. Lou Brock was a common thief (of bases anyway) and

Catfish Hunter had to be, in my 7 year old's opinion, the coolest name in baseball. I had a bunch of cards that would be worth a good amount of money today. At one point, I had over a hundred which was a lot for a second grader!

Back then we hung out with this kid named Harry. Harry was one of those street wise kids that we all looked up to. He was bigger than most of us and had a good sense of humor, even if it was a bit on the dark side. If we were a ragtag gang of punks, Harry was our leader.

Scammed

It was getting to the end of May when Harry came up with a plan to get us all more baseball cards. He got us all together and told us we should all flip with other kids outside our gang and whatever we win we'd give to him to hold. By mid June we had a whole shoe box of cards collected. His idea was to keep going until the last day of school and then we'd split them up between us. There were only four of us (maybe five, it's hard to remember) so we'd each end up with a huge pile. It was going to be great! Each day he'd show us how many cards we all got for the day, and each night we dreamed about the huge pile of cards we'd end up with.

Finally the last day of school came. I could hardly wait. We were all busting at the seams waiting for Harry to get to school. But when he got off the bus, he didn't have the shoe box with him. He didn't have a bag with him. He wasn't carrying anything. He said he forgot the cards at home, but we all knew he was lying. He played us for the naïve, trusting second graders we were. In an instant, everything we worked for was gone, taken in on a ponzi scheme by a kid who called us his friends. We went home that day empty handed and heavy hearted. I never talked to him after that, and I'm not sure what he's up to now but my guess is he's running an investment firm or holds a seat on Wall Street!

Lessons Learned

Of all the important lessons I learned in my life, I think that one was one of my earliest. On that day, I realized the dangers in coveting material things. I let myself get sucked into the notion of treasure only to be slapped down by the emptiness of the treasure chest! Sure, in hindsight it was only baseball cards and for that matter, I wasn't even thinking about the collection value. I just wanted a bigger pile of stuff. I learned the hard way what the Bible warns about when it says not to put your trust in earthly treasures.

Looking back at that incident, I also learned another truth that the Bible shares with us. The truth I'm talking about is the fact that whatever we treasure, our hearts are captured by. It makes perfect sense, doesn't it? Think of the phrase we hear from many a Mom; "My kids are my life." For a lot of parents, their lives absolutely revolve around their children. Between school activities, sports, scouts, band, or a host of untold shared hobbies; parents lives are consumed by providing for, and entertaining their sons and daughters.

I'm a proud parent myself and I remember when my boys were younger. I was always helping them with homework and school projects. They played T-ball, Little League Baseball, Soccer and Basketball, and my youngest even got into Roller Hockey. Half of the teams I helped coach.

They were all in scouting and my oldest went from the rank of Tiger Cub all the way to Eagle. At the Eagle ceremony, the parents were given pins in recognition of all the time and effort they put into helping their sons accomplish this amazing goal. Veteran Scout Masters knew all too well the countless hours parents committed to, along with their children, to make this happen.

Of the whole scouting experience, I have to admit my favorite part was doing the Father-Son cake bakes in Cub Scouts. We made some really amazing cakes; one of the most profitable selling for $75.00. It was a Battleship with tootsie roll cannons modeled after an actual Naval ship that was home for a naval officer the kids were pen-palling with. It was awesome! And if I remember correctly, the officer was actually there and won the bidding war for the cake!

Back then, my own life was dominated by child rearing activities. Whenever I'd talk to people, the conversation always included, if not totaled, updates on what my kids were up to and what the next big adventure was about. Being a parent is all about setting aside your wants and needs until their wants and needs are taken care of. It's a very consuming endeavor, not at all for the self centered or faint of heart!

Defining your Treasure

What captures the lion's share of your thoughts? What would you say you invest the greatest amount of your life in? For some, it's their career. For others, it'll be hobbies and still others, its commercialized sports. (I could say "professional" but commercialized is probably more accurate if you think about it!)

Some people invest most of their energy in financial growth. Every day, they hawk their various investments and massage their portfolios to capture maximum returns. They are in constant study looking for the next big deal that can be flipped into a high profit venture.

There is good logic and sound wisdom in the claim that what you spend the majority of time and attention on is for you, a treasure. To be fair, a career that provides needed income to survive and live comfortably is more of a necessity than a treasure; but for some, their careers are much more than that. Your treasure is typically the thing you are most proud of and the thing you dwell on most in life. Some treasures add to the quality of life while others tend to derail it.

It takes careful planning to align our treasures with success if success is to be measured by love. In the role of parenting, the alignment is seamless by design. God is our parent, we are God's children and as he loves and provides for us, so we try to do the same for our children. The acts of love we give to our children will be carried into eternity because we will continue those acts in Heaven every bit as much as his love continues for us. Apart from that, many of our treasures will be null and void to us on the day we die. They are earthly and temporary.

Think of it this way; if eternity is real and we'll all be part of it one way or the other, what you have today will either be eligible to take with you or it won't. God's recommendation for your eternal happiness is to invest in treasures that will be eligible to take with you into eternity. Does this mean it's wrong to be a N.Y. Jets fan? Of course it is, but that's beside the point! (Sorry; inside joke to all my friends and family keeping the faith for the Jets!) The real point is that there's nothing wrong with being a sports fan or an investment wizard, or the best at your hobby or career, as long as that's not what defines your purpose in life. If any of those do define your purpose in life, then you won't have a purpose to bring with you into eternity.

If loving God and loving others is your primary purpose, and you choose to act out your love through your career or hobby, then I believe you will be able to carry those actions into eternity. It might be different in specifics but it will be the same in nature. One example of a loving career is nursing. God bless these people! They are some of the finest human beings on earth. Another may be the military. God absolutely honors those who put their lives on the line for the safety and security of others. But in both of these cases, the specific career may not be practiced in Heaven since there won't be either sickness or war. I believe God will provide alternative jobs that will fulfill the desires of these people who live to lovingly serve others.

Perspective

If you're like me, you don't particularly care for what you're doing as a career. I currently work at IBM in a Lithography area making microchips. Was that my life long dream? Nope! I spend a substantial chunk of my life there but would I consider it my treasure? No I wouldn't. But when people ask me who I work for, I don't say IBM, I say God. I consider my workplace to be a mission field and my work ethic to be a witness and I deeply appreciate the privilege of this employment. I thank God every day for giving me a way to share his love while providing for my family.

It doesn't matter what you're doing to make a buck as much as how you view your opportunity. I've done a lot of different kinds of work, some I love and some I never want to do again. I do know that no matter what I do to make money now, the real employer is God. He is the one who meets my daily needs, even if it's through earthly suppliers. If you want a morale boost for your job, I suggest working for God. With him as your boss, pretty much anything we have to do here is tolerable.

Everything we do in life can be viewed the same way. Whether it's doing laundry, changing the oil on your car, or cooking for your family; think about it in terms of working for God. Always remember that God uses ordinary people like you and I every day to fulfill his will. It doesn't have to be anything as big as starting a church or writing a book; those things are great but so are washing dishes and taking out the garbage if you're doing it for God. And if everything you're doing is for God, then guess where your treasure is?

So enjoy your kids for God. Make microchips for God. You can even watch the Jets game for God and it would be doing him a favor, because even God in all his power and patience can endure only so much pain! (Yeah...I went there again!)

When God is your foundation, and loving him is the underlying purpose for all that you do, life is good! When you have a heart after God, your treasure is always safe, no matter what happens. Never forget that we only take our souls to Heaven when we leave. Earthly treasures are fun and meant to be enjoyed; otherwise God wouldn't put them here. However, we should make sure our eternal treasures are stored up first, so that when we have to let go of this life, we are all the more happy to embrace the next.

At this point you'd be right to ask the common sense question; "But what are *eternal treasures*?" In the physical realm we collect things we like; things we feel add to our quality of life. Money is probably one of the most popular examples of physical treasure because, with it, you can purchase almost any other physical thing. But in the spiritual realm we have the unique opportunity as human beings to be very rich without a penny to our name. That's because spiritual wealth is something you build up in your heart and not your bank account. My humble opinion is that spiritual currency far outweighs anything of value in the physical realm.

When balancing the spiritual tallyman's scales of worth,

we are faced with hard questions to answer. What is the value of honor? How about wisdom? What does it cost for an ounce of honesty or a pound of compassion? What do the scales tell us about valor or self sacrifice? When is enough forgiveness counted as enough? What is the weight of love when it's purified by God? Is it measured in Mother's tears or Father's pride? Is there even a scale that can hold the weight of all the pain we suffer for those we love? Is there rope strong enough to tie down the joy we share on their behalf? I can probably recite a ton of verses from the books of Proverbs or Psalms that would answer some of these questions plainly, but I'd rather cover them with another question.

When thinking about worth in a physical way, we often think about what other people consider valuable. We consider the things most people want. For the spiritual treasures I would suggest we take a similar approach. What does God really want? What would *He* consider valuable? I could say "Obedience" but I don't think that captures it well enough. For the answer to these questions, I'd like to reference the book of Micah. Micah seems to hit the nail squarely on its head in chapter 6, verses 6-8. There Micah compares the physical treasures of the day to the spiritual treasures God really wants;

> With what shall I come before the LORD
> and bow down before the exalted God?
> Shall I come before him with burnt offerings,
> with calves a year old?

Will the LORD be pleased with thousands of rams,
with ten thousand rivers of oil?
Shall I offer my firstborn for my transgression,
the fruit of my body for the sin of my soul?

He has showed you, O man, what is good.
And what does the LORD require of you?
To act justly and to love mercy
and to walk humbly with your God.

Pretty much every good and pure character trait can be found and developed in practicing those three basic "treasures" for God. Act justly, love mercy and walk humbly! For a God who holds the universe in the palm of his hands, these are the things he wants. When we view these character traits in that perspective, we can easily see how very wealthy we can become in the spiritual realm.

How much would you pay to have a real, deep and abiding relationship with a loving God? Would you pay a thousand, ten thousand or a million? Actually it's a trick question! We don't pay to have a relationship with God; He pays us! I know it sounds like a "gimmicky" sales pitch to say that, with God, we can "earn while we learn" but in the eternal treasures market, that's exactly what we do. When we allow God to lead us and teach us; as we humble ourselves and allow our weakness to give way to his strength, we grow treasures in Heaven and enlarge God's kingdom.

Suffering takes many forms. Pain can be physical, mental or emotional. Sacrifice seems to be a bottomless pit at times. But when everything we do, we do for the glory of God, not one tear or sting or loss, however small or large, is wasted. It is all counted as righteousness and treasure for God that he promises to lavish on us when we are called home. I know these words seem to imply that living for God is definitely going to bring pain. If truth be told, love is a two edged sword that we can't experience without dealing with, or even inviting some level of pain into our lives. But let's be honest; when we consider life without God and love as experienced through him, it would seem all we're left with is a painful emptiness.

I don't like being hurt, and when I look back at the canvas of my life, I clearly see images of pain that, to this day invoke a sting in my heart. But it doesn't end with that. I immediately feel the love of God again, because he helped me through those times. I am instantly reminded of the valuable lessons I've learned as my mind is filled with all the traps and snares that I've avoided because I was blessed with certain trials in my life.

It's been a lifetime since I learned my second grade lesson about wanting more stuff. But every day I learn more about the greatness of God's eternal treasures. I pray that he continues to guide my heart to hold loosely to earthly things and instead, hold tightly to things that last forever. And every day that I put Him first is a day that I am very richly blessed!

Calling All Saints

"One tear in the driving rain, one voice in a sea of pain, can the maker of the stars hear the sound of my breaking heart?"
Tenth Avenue North

Of all the opportunities we have to love people, one of the greatest actions we can take is to help them carry their burdens with prayer. Whenever we use prayer to partner with those in need, we are practicing the most basic form of love. To understand this better we need to think about what prayer actually is; feelings of good intention expressed through words of faith that God has the power to enact change.

Johns' Gospel opens with a simple yet profound truth; "In the beginning was the Word." Why does John label Jesus with such a basic title? A "word" to us is a tool to express a thought, be it an idea or a description of something.

I like to interpret this as meaning that, even before any creation came into being; God cared in an expressible way for us and all creation. His love was already transferable to us and the venue he chose to express it was the spoken word. And speak he did, for everything created was spoken into existence.

The Bible doesn't say that God grabbed some heavenly tools and built stuff. He didn't draw up a ton of plans, take a pile of clay and sculpt plants and animals to breathe into. The Word simply said, "Let there be" and there was! This truth is a breaking point for many a scientific minded soul. They can't get their heads around this creative ability and quite frankly, as unbelievable as it is, who can blame them. Some would say that this is where faith comes in but I would go a step further. We need to remove the idea of faith for this application and replace it with the words *Humility* and *Trust*. Humility helps us with the realization that there are much bigger and stronger forces at work than we can ever understand. Trust is the tool we use to bridge the gap between knowing we can't understand something and admitting that there's someone who can.

The Importance of Belief

One of the biggest blocks to my faith growing up was that if I was going to believe in something, it had to be believable to me. Too many kind hearted people told me that we'll never understand spiritual things and we should just accept them by faith. That doesn't carry a very sound argument and does nothing to promote a healthy spiritual life. While there are spiritual mysteries we may never resolve on this side of Heaven, there are many things we can prove out and build our faith upon. If you do your homework you will find that Science, History and Christianity compliment, far more than contradict each other. Our faith shouldn't be considered a blind admittance as much as an educated confession.

There are many books available on Apologetics that clearly explain to the lay reader, why Christianity is a sound belief system that does not require us to check our brains at the door. If you're at all serious about your spiritual health, I strongly suggest you do a study of Christian Apologetics so that you can explain to yourself, if no one else, why you believe in the facts presented in the historical records of the Holy Bible.

One excellent resource to begin with would be Lee Strobel's "A Case for..." series. Lee Strobel was a confessed atheist who set out to disprove the validity of Christianity. Lee was a respected Journalist who enjoyed high honors in his field for his work as an Investigative Reporter, before accepting a position as Legal Editor for the Chicago Tribune. He had the clout and excellent resources to perform a detailed analysis of the facts. As an Atheist he thought he knew the facts for not believing in God so he began with focusing his research on the contrary group; experts who did believe in God.

What he found was a mound of strong evidence supporting biblical claims while uncovering very real loopholes in what the secular world teaches as scientific fact. These findings compelled him to rethink his own belief system. As he dug deeper into the evidence and sifted out the proven vs. theoretical on both sides of the Science-Religion fence, he found that these opposing sides actually feathered together in harmony more times than not.

Even with all the extensive investigations that Mr. Strobel and many of the scientists and theologians he interviewed have done, there are still a lot of questions to be answered. What we need to have as seekers is enough humility to recognize that there may be many things we don't understand now, but that doesn't mean they aren't true. We trust that quantum physics is real, but how many of us can explain it? We've seen the destructive power of hatred and the healing of forgiveness, but can anyone fully understand human nature and why we do the things we do?

At some point we are forced to face the fact that we don't know some things and we're going to have to trust them to someone who knows more then us. We see this in every field we deal with from accounting to auto repair. Why wouldn't it apply to spiritual matters? What kind of god would be worthy of worship and awe if humans could eventually figure out every mystery ourselves? Only foolish pride would entertain the thought that we could ever figure it all out. As valid as the scientific method is, we have no right to say that unless it's provable, it's not real. No one can prove how or why all of creation came into being and even the most ardent atheist scientists admit they may never know.

Despite what the liberal education system claims, nothing uncovered in science can accurately explain the origin of life. At this point it all boils down to two opposing thoughts; Evolution and Intelligent Design. Evolution dictates that there is no real purpose to life or pre-planned reason for our existence. It poses theories about the origin of life but they have been discredited by the facts found through the scientific method. Intelligent design dictates that for reasons yet unknown, all of creation does have a purpose and a design to suit that purpose. In total agreement with science, intelligent design states that all effects have a cause. Something caused the creation to happen. The fact that we can't scientifically prove what that is yet doesn't mean it's not real.

For many of us Bible believers on the planet, we take all the incredible volumes of evidence found and proven to be true and we stack it up against the few unknowns still out there to be explained. As Lee Strobel expresses in his book "A Case for Faith", on balance, realizing that there's more than enough proven evidence in support of a loving God, we choose to believe and humbly trust that he knows what he's doing. We choose to believe that there is a Creator with the power, as mysterious as it is, to speak us into existence; and I'm sure that when we meet him face to face, he will help us understand all the science behind it.

The Power of Our Words

Since we were created in God's image, we too were meant to speak, with our hearts and minds, if not with our mouths.

Even if we are utterly helpless in every physical way to promote a change of circumstances for hurting souls, we have the power to move mountains for them in the spiritual realms. This power is astonishingly efficient and when used in a selfless way for good, is always honored by God.

As a loving mother gives her child exactly what they need when they need it, so too God provides for us in our times of need when we respectfully ask. It may not be to our desire or timing but it's always what is best for us and always at the right time. However, I believe there is a caveat to Gods' obligation to answer our prayers.

My personal feeling is that God always wants to help us, but we live lives devoid of his presence until we realize we need him. We sometimes create scenarios where we have bigger issues to fix than the ones we're consumed in prayer with. God, being who he is, sees our more important needs from an eternal perspective and works in our lives to fix them first. Unfortunately, our selfish nature often blocks our spiritual eyes from seeing the positive in our physically negative situation and we turn away from God rather then closer toward him. We refuse to seek him or follow his will because we don't understand it. Yet, if we truly stop our own direction and have faith in his eternal plan; if we can find a way to trust him for our own sake, we will eventually find the light at the end of the dark tunnel we're in. We might not understand this now but we will in time, if we step toward him in faith.

There are many types of prayers that we can say; some

are formally scripted while others border on total gibberish as the Holy Spirit takes over and vocally speaks through us. I have no biblical basis for my opinion but I'd bet God mostly enjoys us just plain talking to him.

Praying to God in conversation blesses him and demonstrates our love for him. It allows us to drop our guard and get close to him. Anyone who has children can appreciate the times when a child comes up and just wants to talk. I don't mean idle chit-chat but rather when they come to you with a deep concern that they feel only your wisdom can resolve. Wouldn't it be nice to always have the wisdom they need from you? You can get it from God. He knows exactly what you need far better than you do.

The Bible says that Wisdom cries out at the city gates calling for anyone to come and be taught. Praying for wisdom is like doing push ups; the more you do, the stronger you'll get. It really is as simple as it says; "Ask and you will receive. Seek and you will find. Knock and the door will open for you." God wants us to receive his wisdom so that we can better recognize his will and align our hearts and minds to his.

God loves it when we talk to him about anything. He wants to be the center of our lives no matter what condition our lives are in. His shoulders are big and he can take any problem you have; but do both of you a favor and bring more than just your problems. Bring him everything! Tell him what you want and what you don't want. Tell him how you feel about cultural issues, political issues and financial issues and yes, even issues of love. He especially wants to help you with your relationships.

Of all the things God created, I imagine relationships are his greatest joy. He takes every opportunity he can to love us and help us to love one another through relationships. Second only to free will; relationship is a very key ingredient to the success of love! You can't love if you're always alone. You certainly can't love to the level you were made to, without a relationship with God. Conversation is an important tool for how we relate to God, and relate to each other.

Remember that every conversation has two sides. As much as he wants to hear your side, he wants you to hear his! But how would we do that? The best way is to read his word! I've read the Bible a dozen times or more and it always amazes me when the very thing I'm going through and praying to him about ends up exactly right there in the section I'm just coming to at the time.

Even more astounding is the fact that the same verse that spoke to me ten years ago about what I was dealing with then, now speaks a whole new message about what I'm dealing with now. Ask anyone who reads the Bible on a regular basis and they'll say the same thing. I'm not making this up; listening to God through his word is always applicable to your current life issues. You'd think that the culture of biblical times would be vastly different then today's culture but it's surprising to see how human nature hasn't changed very much.

When We Ask

"Request" prayers are probably the most common type of prayer and the kind most people practice. Believe it or not, praying in petition for others is as much a benefit to us as it is to them. Each time we lift up others in prayer it strengthens our relationship with God; blessing him through our obedience to love others, while training our hearts and minds to be closer to his. When we care enough for those in need to carry their concerns to God in prayer, we reflect his selfless nature. In turn God, seeing our capacity for love growing, fills us all the more with his loving spirit. We will never be able to out-love God but we can expand our hearts to make more room for his love to reach others through us.

One day I was dwelling heavily on the concept of loving people as God loves them. I couldn't conceive of a way that I could even begin to do that until he laid it on my heart to pray for them. He brought the word "investment" to mind. In the last chapter I spoke about where our treasures are, so our hearts are also. God showed me that if I really wanted to have a heart of love for other people then I should start investing in them. At first I didn't understand. I got the part about treating my neighbors as I'd treat myself, but what about all people? What about people I'll never meet? How can I possibly love all of them, especially in a way that resembles how God loves them?

I can't recall why I was there but I was at an airport terminal, watching all these people walking by; people from all walks of life, every age and race, passing by on their way to wherever they were going. As I sat and watched, God's still small voice whispered to my heart. "These are all my children and I love all of them as much as I love you. Pray for them!"

With my imagination filling in the blanks, I began to speak in my mind prayers for every face I could capture as each person walked by. There was a mom with a baby in a stroller and luggage in tow and I asked God to give her strength for the journey and rest on the plane. A man in a business suit walked by and I prayed that God would bless his business with fairness and endurance. A young couple, apparently college students acting conspicuously carefree, prompted me to pray that God would bless them with courage for the challenges they are facing. On and on it went, for many minutes and many more people. I prayed for every face I saw, imagining where they were going, not just on a plane but in life. As I prayed I could feel my heart caring more and more for these strangers that I'd never meet.

Through the ongoing experience I believed that God was listening and honoring my requests, not because anyone deserved special treatment but because I was taking the time to love them for God. I could imagine the smile on his face as I worked to keep up, catching as many people with my prayer net as I could. Eventually I stopped, and when I did I found myself exhausted by the effort but at the same time exhilarated in spirit.

I return to that exercise now and again, in the supermarket or at work; especially at work. I spend a lot of time with the same group of people day after day and to be honest, I don't know even half of their names. Still, every once in a while, as I look at someone, I can see a strain in their face as if an invisible burden is strapped to their back like that of Christian's in the story "Pilgrims' Progress." I instantly begin to pray for them without even knowing what I'm praying for. It's as if God is sending an instant message to my heart, "PFT! TX!, ILU, BFF" It's always an honor to lift up my coworkers in prayer. I consider it to be the real reason I'm there, to love them for God. It's kind of funny but on a few occasions, I had the opportunity to pray for people's needs with them, not two seconds after they expressed the need. You can see the surprise in their faces when people just get to work caring for them on the spot like that. It's an action of real-time love that always brings relief and hope to their faces.

Calm in the Storm

One particular prayer petition that I was much honored to participate in was on the fateful day of September 11th, 2001. I was working that day at the IBM East Fishkill, NY Manufacturing Fab. There were roughly a hundred of us there that day when the news started trickling in; a small plane crashed into one of the towers; no, it was actually a big plane, a commercial airliner. We started hitting the Web for news but the internet was bogged down and information was coming in slow. Then rumors started spreading about the plane being hijacked. Another plane was reported crashing into the other tower; still more news came about other planes in the air that may be hijacked as well. A plane struck the Pentagon. Another plane crashed in the woods somewhere in Pennsylvania. The Fab floor was consumed with panic and fear.

While some people spoke of leaving, others sat stunned at the prospects and uncertainty of it all. Management came in, equally shaken and gave the canned answers provided them which were not to panic; do your jobs and try to stay calm. Assessments were made whether anyone had family in the air or in one of the Twin Towers. Anyone directly connected was free to leave and do whatever they thought they needed to. Some of us asked management if we could have an emergency meeting to get everyone on the same page and try to calm some nerves but they said that wouldn't be happening. I remember feeling so absolutely helpless.

While some prayed by themselves and others prayed in small groups, many wandered aimlessly, obviously not accustomed to praying much at all, but not knowing what to grab onto for hope or reassurance of any kind. It hurt me to see such anguish in all their faces. I felt someone had to do something and it seemed those in authority had no plans other then to attempt to act normal.

I started spreading the word about a prayer meeting in a nearby conference room. It would be at 1:00pm and anyone who wished could come. I asked that people don't tell management so that they couldn't officially call it off. I had a little over an hour to pull together a list of high ranking officials that I felt would be extremely burdened by this obvious terrorist attack. I listed by names; the President, the Vice President and the Secretary of State, the Secretary of Defense, the Governor of New York as well as the Mayor of N.Y. City. I even added the names of top generals that I could find that would no doubt be involved in our country's response.

I sat in the conference room at 12:45pm so that I could pray alone in preparation. I asked God for wisdom and calmness. I prayed for the ability to speak clearly and concisely so that everyone could hear. Most of all I prayed for courage, for myself and my co-workers, to make it through the rest of the shift without totally breaking down. At about 12:55pm, people started shuffling in. The conference room held forty people comfortably. By the time we started around 1:05pm, the room was packed tightly; standing room only. I would be remiss if I did not say how very proud I was of all my co-workers for standing together in a time of such desperate spiritual need.

Since it was my idea to have the gathering, I felt responsible to guide it. I thanked everyone for coming and asked that we begin. We started by acknowledging God's presence in the midst of this tragedy and thanked him for always being there at such trying times as these in life. We prayed for God to accept all those who lost their lives in this tragedy. We asked that his blessed peace and strength be given to all the families and friends that had loved ones unaccounted for, whether in the towers, the Pentagon or on one of the planes that crashed that day. We asked for courage and strength for those now strapped with the overwhelming task of search and rescue. I then read off, by name and title, all the officials I had gathered on the list, that they may have his wisdom, courage and compassion in the days and weeks ahead as they deal with this terrible event.

We ended the prayer by first asking that God be with us on this day that none of us would ever forget, as we attempted to sift out all the confusion our feeling were raging though. And then, to bring everyone together in a tangible way, I ended with the familiar words; "Lord help us to pray as you have taught us...Our father, who art in Heaven...". With that everyone in the room broke into the soft silence and joined in reciting the Lord's Prayer.

When we were done, many of us were crying, hugging and trying to be supportive of each other. It was obvious that the restrictive bind of confusion and terror was now broken, allowing people to begin working through this newly inflicted pain we shared. Through prayer, God's love released us in a way no other power could do.

As the collective spirit of our nation continued to struggle through the reverberating waves of stress, pain and sorrow, many reached up in prayer. Places of worship opened their doors daily to a frightened and angry nation and through it all, God helped stabilize our fears and temper our anger. As much as we wanted to hate, he helped us to love. Never in my life have I seen such an outpouring of renewed faith and seeking of God.

Helping Kids Cope

The following week my son and I attended an annual prayer event called "See You at The Pole". SYATP started back in 1990 in Burleson, Texas with a small group of teens who felt burdened to pray for their communities. They decided to drive to three different schools one night to pray for their friends, their schools and those in leadership. Since then the prayer movement has grown exponentially. Today millions of students across all fifty states as well as at least twenty other countries meet on the fourth Wednesday of September before school starts. They gather around the school flag pole and pray for everyone from friends and family to faculty to local, state and federal government leaders.

In 2001, the event was still being held on the third Wednesday of the month and it fell on September 19th. My son and I arrived along with a handful of others and gathered around the flag pole and began to pray. The weather was calm, partly cloudy and a bit cool as it usually is towards the end of September in upstate New York. We had gotten there just before buses started rolling in and enjoyed a brief period of quiet reflection and prayer. At first there were only about eight of us. We held hands and formed a circle around the pole and took turns reciting what was on our hearts.

As our small collection of prayer warriors continued, teens poured into the area from buses and cars, walking past us. At first, some kids would stop, curious to see what we were doing, while others walked past with nothing more than a quick glance. But as the minutes clicked by, the weight of the times drew more and more to pause.

I like to close my eyes when I pray. It helps me to concentrate on what I'm thinking, feeling and saying. Shortly after we started, I closed my eyes and tried to drift into a heart of worship and humility before God. The prayers lasted for about fifteen minutes. We all took turns around this small inner circle, vocally expressing our fears and concerns to God, asking for his protection and wisdom.

In previous years the gathering was, for the most part, uneventful in nature. We'd congregate, pray, and then go about our day thankful for the opportunity, even if it was just a handful of us. But this time was different. When we finished praying I opened my eyes to see that we were literally surrounded by what looked like over a hundred teens, standing with tear filled eyes; holding each others' hands; hugging and praying, reaching for God for maybe the first time in their lives. I was stunned to see it all. The spiritual need was palpable as the sense of loss and confusion these kids carried just hung in the air. Like the people I prayed with at work eight days earlier, these kids were desperate for God's comfort in this terrifying time of national crisis. They needed to know that God was there, that he was listening and that he still cared about America.

Prayer got a lot of us through that very trying time. Prayer continues to help many people across the globe cope with the tangled mess of natural and man made disasters. God is always waiting to listen to us. His love is available 24/7/365. When we call on him in prayer we are saying that we trust him and need him. When we lift others in prayer we are saying that we love them enough to trust him with their needs and trust in his providence, even if we may not understand how or why it works.

We are to love God with all our heart, all our soul, all our strength and our entire mind; and we are to love our neighbors as ourselves. In God's view we are all neighbors on a small planet. From his point of view it's far simpler than we are making it to be. The capacity we have for fear rules over our capacity to love. Our selfishness drowns out our ability to naturally do for others as we would want them to do for us. It may be a huge investment to house a homeless person or give a neighbor enough money for a months' worth of groceries but we can at least begin to love by investing time to pray for them.

If we compare the amount of time we spend watching television with the amount of time we pray for others, surely we'll see that we can love others a little bit more and ourselves a little bit less. That's all God is asking of us. With all he's done for us, that's the very least that we can do. To love others as we love ourselves may seem like an unreasonable or unachievable command, but it isn't. God never asks us to do things we can't.

We have a very long way to go to get where God would have us, but we do have a way to begin the journey for change. It's a starting point we can all afford. If you want to begin loving others as you love yourself, then pray for them today!

You Are What You Think

"The world we have created is a product of our thinking; it cannot be changed without changing our thinking"
Albert Einstein

A lot of people think they have a lot to say about a lot of things. I Googled the phrase "you are what you think" and came up with over 500 million results. That's a lot of results on the topic of thinking. The acts of people thinking about thinking are as old as dirt and people who get paid to tell us how to think are as plentiful as the sands of the Sahara. As I sit and watch television these days I can't help but wonder what the media thinks we should be thinking about. I shudder to think about what my great grandchildren will be exposed to.

It seems to me that we're taught a lot of things we have no business dwelling on, while forsaking things that would strengthen our character. We trade in valor for violence and sanctity for smut. We're bored with decency and captivated with indiscretion. If truth be told, a lot of the content of our American sitcoms is anything but funny when you really think about it.

One of my all time favorite movie quotes was the line from Jurassic Park when Dr. Ian Malcolm, a Chaos Theorist argued against the ill fated idea of cloning dinosaurs. As John Hammond, the park owner, bragged about the genius of his science team in the cloning process, Dr. Malcolm stated "Yeah, but your scientists were so preoccupied with whether or not they could, they never stopped to think about if they should." In theatrical retrospect, I'd say they probably shouldn't have; at the very least they could have skipped cloning the raptors!

The idea of cloning is a hot topic for some. On the left you have the argument for the ability to replicate useable human parts that can save lives; on the right you have the grave concern (no pun intended) over the state of a soul or lack thereof in a cloned human being. It's fundamentally a question of people playing God compounded by the fact that the people on the left in this case don't necessarily believe in any god, thus thinking it doesn't make any sense not to pursue cloning. For the record I side with Ian Malcolm and say it's a very bad idea. I imagine there's a limit to what God will tolerate and this type of science may be it!

Ignoring the Right vs. Wrong Factor

The truth in Malcolm's statement is in the fact that people sometimes follow an idea without really thinking it through to the end. When we dismiss the "right or wrong" in what we think about, we set ourselves up for a terrible fall. I would argue that we've not given enough attention to the levels of immorality our culture has allowed, to the detriment of our national character and reputation. It would be prudent to think about where we're going and where this road of relativism is taking us.

There are a lot of wonderful ideas that science and business successfully translate into practical applications. God has blessed many a mind with good things to think of to meet the needs of his children. Throughout the ages, people of all nations have discovered medicines, invented machines and reasoned for peace over violence. We've penned mathematical proofs and literary brilliance. While there's real beauty in living a simple, technically minimalist lifestyle, I do appreciate the creative genius that today's technology expresses; but whether Amish or Astrophysicist, we can all honor God with our thoughts and the wisdom he gives us.

One problem facing the human race is that a lot of powerful people seem to forget or ignore the fact that truly healthy wisdom and thoughts are from God. One of God's most beautiful creatures fell into this trap long ago and now Lucifer uses his God given power and wisdom for our destruction. He has whispered into the ear of many a world leader causing the darkest stains to appear on the pages of human history.

What makes us so quick to turn our backs on God's instruction, thinking we know what's best for ourselves? Surely human curiosity was never meant to linger so long at the dark things in life; yet with the absence of God's light in our lives, darkness is all that we are left with. Maybe it's a fundamental infatuation with power itself, so easy to see in a destructive force yet harder to detect in the slower creative processes it inhabits? I'll admit I like watching a tornado video more than a video on the migration of turtles. There's something about seeing such catastrophic destruction displayed in the power of a twister. Would I be as fascinated if the twister went around planting trees instead of yanking them out of the ground?

Think of the amazing amount of energy it must take to grow a forest; all the interconnected biological processes that execute flawlessly over years of time to make such a wonderful habitat. We probably don't think much about all that it takes to make a forest; in fact we more often liken it to watching grass grow! On the other hand, I'm sure all of us have thought plenty on the destructive power of a forest fire or volcanic eruption that turns the decades of natural work to wasteland in a matter of hours. Somehow destruction appears more powerful and it intrigues us. Why are our minds so captivated by such things?

God knows how our minds work because he designed them. He gave us the gift of curiosity so that we would grow intellectually. He gives us his wisdom so that we can use our intellect to bless him and bless each other. We were created to use his light as our guide but unfortunately we sometimes drift our sight away from his light and into the darkness. We are tricked into thinking that if we let go of his hand we can easily stay in the light by ourselves but we can't. Our pride pulls us away as our eyes adjust to the darkness. Before we know it we can see in the darkness to the degree that it seems painful to look into the light again; so we squint and turn away from the things of God and think more about the things of this world.

The effects of Exposure

If our mind's eye is the guide for our steps in life, do we do enough to protect what we allow it to view? If a picture is truly worth a thousand words, doesn't it stand to reason that what we see could have a strong influence on how we think? Could repeated exposure to violence promote apathy for it? Is there a correlation between all the sex on TV and the unbelievable rise in teen pregnancy?

I'm not a psychologist or a statistician but I'd bet the more of something you expose people to, the more acceptable to them it becomes over time. A good case study for this is the Homosexual movement in America. Homosexuality is nothing new by any stretch, and I imagine there's been some level of homosexual activity in this country since its inception. What is relatively new is a cultural acceptance of it.

I admit I'm one of those people who have absolutely no homosexual tendencies and cannot relate at all to how two people of the same gender are so sexually attracted to each other. Whether it's right or wrong was never my call to make; it's God's decision. He makes it very clear that homosexuality is wrong. He also makes it very clear that lying is wrong, coveting is wrong, being judgmental is wrong and we should never dishonor our parents, yet I doubt there's a human being alive today who hasn't done at least one of these things or something else that God clearly defines as wrong. In the eyes of God we are all sinners; so I don't single out homosexuality as a "worse" sin than anything that I've done.

The point I make is that homosexuality seems to be extremely pervasive in today's television programming to the point that we even have homosexuals in commercials now. There's no mistaking the reason for this. Our culture, in the view of the liberal media, needs to be desensitized and made more accepting of homosexuality. By making us think about it more, we should eventually all come to accept it more; or at least that's the plan. The problem is that, for people like me who cannot relate to their same sex attraction, it will always be "queer" to us; meaning weird, unnatural and not normal.

As a Christian I have to ask myself what God wants me to think of homosexuals. What does God's word say about what things we should think about in relation to life and all we encounter in it, be it good or bad? Philippians 4:8 spells it out as clearly as can be said;

> "Finally, brothers, whatever is true, whatever is noble, whatever is right, whatever is pure, whatever is lovely, whatever is admirable – if anything is excellent or praiseworthy – think about such things."

The obvious conclusion is that God says not to dwell on homosexuality. I think He'd have us not dwell on sex at all; rather dwell on things that are excellent and praiseworthy. Sex, in and of itself, isn't a bad thing. God's word clearly explains the blessings of sex when practiced within the boundaries of marriage between a man and a woman. He designed us to be sexual beings for a purpose, and that's to draw us into a loving relationship that promotes creation. It's just like him to make it so much fun!

Sex itself, on the other hand, is not something that deserves as much attention as we give it. God wants our thoughts to be on things that lift our character to a higher level. We're not to be known for our sexual orientation, but for how we love and serve our fellow man. Sexual orientation is at best a personal thing. It's not meant to define us. Some people present the argument that if God created all things and controls all things, then why did he make people with homosexual tendencies? I would put forth that God didn't create people with homosexual tendencies but rather they were born into a sinful world, run by an evil spirit who is more than happy to inflict people with homosexual tendencies. Deep down, anyone who truly seeks God must face the truth that God doesn't approve of it.

The problem in America is that there are a lot of ungodly people in control of the media and education who are products of the 'sexual revolution" that America went through in the last few decades. They are children of the "Me" generation. But how are sincere Christians supposed to deal with our cultural confusion?

Here's a practical example: You have neighbors that are homosexual. They are hard working, very loving people, respected in the community for volunteer work and attend church regularly. You on the other hand have never done any volunteer work and have a slight drinking problem. You're a good Dad to your children and you clearly demonstrate love and respect for your wife. You attend church regularly but only because it's a good way to network for your sales job. What would God have me think of you both? I believe he would want me to see you both as children of God just like me, doing well in some parts of life and struggling in others. He would not want me to point out the splinters in your eyes since I have a plank in my own. He would want me to simply love you all as I love myself.

Most of us on this side of Heaven are either in denial or unaware of sins we commit. We're naturally self protective and self bias. Yet we have little problem in seeing the imperfections of others. Instead of standing in judgment of one another, we should be looking for ways to bring out the best in each other. That starts with keeping God out in front of us. God doesn't want me to dwell on your drinking problem or their homosexuality. He'd much rather I dwell on how I can love you both with the gifts he gave me to use. Please don't get me wrong; I'm not saying we should ignore the sins of others by putting our heads in the sand. What I am saying is that while I feel I have the obligation to disagree with either neighbor on what's acceptable, I am first and foremost called to love them without judgment; especially if judgment keeps forcing me to dwell on sinful things.

Changing our Minds

We need to rethink what we all think about. To begin doing that we need to put God first in our lives; slip the lens of God in front of our hearts and pray for his Holy Spirit to guide us with his wisdom. Only then will the veil be lifted so we can see how far into the dark we've strayed. Only then will things that are true, noble, right, pure, lovely, admirable and praiseworthy seem excellent to us. This isn't an easy thing to do these days; television is enemy number one and the internet is a very close second. We need to be deliberate about what we watch and what we refuse to watch because, like it or not, it shapes the way we think about, and ultimately treat each other.

The same thing applies to music. I love rock music, especially when it's fused with blues, rap, country or whatever. I grew up with everyone from Cat Stevens and Jackson Browne to Eric Clapton, Van Halen, Led Zeppelin and my once favorite band, Yes! I love the style of Linkin Park and I believe Nirvana was a total game changer for the face of rock. I prefer listening to music over watching TV anytime. When I gave my life to Christ I made a decision to convert to Contemporary Christian music. I'm not trying to lay a guilt trip on anyone for listening to the above mentioned bands; it was just my way of showing God how serious I was for him. I need to say however that until I gave my life to Christ, I never realized how dark some secular music was getting.

I remember one early Sunday morning, driving to work and flipping through the radio dial, I was trying to find some good music and I hit the preset for a local secular station. The station had a Sunday morning Christian Rock hour that I never heard before. It was the first time I had ever heard the band "DC Talk," a Rap/Rock group with three young men totally sold out for God and Rap music. I was blown away. I had never heard anything like it. Shortly after that I received in the mail an invitation to join Columbia House. Remember them? It was how you got music cheap before the internet was invented.

I had no idea what bands to pick because I didn't know any and I didn't have any Christian friends to ask. I had a lot of friends that said they were Christian, but they really weren't. I went for the "14 tapes for 99 cents" deal and picked the bands by genre and description; and so it began. I was amazed at how these Christian bands had the same hard driving guitars and raging vocals as my secular music, but had a much better message. Since then I've amassed quite a collection.

If you like James Taylor then you'll love Jim Cole. If you like Eminem then give KJ-52 a try. If Linkin Park is your style, give Pillar and P.O.D. a shot. You will not be disappointed. There are Christian bands or soloists for every taste and genre. While some breathe fresh air into the old hymns, others take it to the very edge screaming hard questions to God and pointing back to his love and mercy for answers.

Listening to Christian music is like bringing church right into your home or car or wherever you go with your MP3 player. It's a way to keep your faith strong every day. For parents, it's an excellent way to help teens stay on a good course. The lyrics reinforce Philippians 4:8 and help them keep their minds on things that are pure and true and praiseworthy. More importantly, it keeps them from constantly turning to the "Idols" of this world that spew Gangsta Rap, Death Grunge or X Rated Pop. We are all collectively responsible for shaping their young minds and hearts. We need to feed them with good thoughts; not destructive ones. Contemporary Christian music is the "health food" their minds need, to keep them positive in today's negative culture.

There's no way we can be with our kids one hundred percent of the time, so it's crucial that we teach them to protect themselves from bad influences. The same applies to adults we care about. A lot of people grossly under estimate the dangers of allowing bad thoughts and influences into their minds. Media is to our minds what light is to our eyes. When you're in the light, your eyes adjust to it and you are comfortable and can see things clearly. If you step into a dark room, your eyes will eventually adjust to the darkness and you will be comfortable with that but you'll struggle to see things clearly. The darkness has a way of playing tricks on your vision. Today's media plays the same kind of tricks on our thoughts.

We need to stay in the light. We need to allow God to fill our minds with honorable things. We need to help each other stay away from bad influences and get excited about being good influences in this world. We covet what we see. It's human nature. Let's make it a point to seek out things that are pure and lovely, rather than twisted and dark. Let's read and write stories of honor and nobility rather than tragedy and hopelessness. Trade in the slasher movie for one the classic "feel good" movies of the year. It's OK to cry at a movie as long as no one sees you! You can still rock hard, just choose to do it with lyrics that lift you up rather than hold you down. You can rap without bustin' a cap if you know what I mean.

With much freedom comes much responsibility. We need to stop being a nation that demands all the freedoms without taking up the responsibility that goes with it. I'm all for free speech and freedom of expression but if our creative skills continue to take us down an ever darkening road then maybe we should rethink what we're allowing for the sake of freedom.

If violent crime, rape and murder statistics are any measure, then I vote for some censorship. It would be unfortunate, but it seems we are losing more and more control as the generations pass; all the while our hearts and minds are being dulled to the hazards, as our national apathy grows. I think it's high time we get a grip on ourselves and our culture before we turn our country into a cesspool of filth that is unbecoming of the great nation we were meant to be! Our forefathers worked too hard and sacrificed too much for us to lead the country down such a disgraceful path. It's time we wake up from our slumber party and get back to a responsible reality!

Letting Go

"He who is devoid of the power to forgive is devoid of the power to love. There is some good in the worst of us and some evil in the best of us. When we discover this, we are less prone to hate our enemies."
Martin Luther King

If love is anything, it's forgiving. I once backed into a friend's car ever so slightly. Lucky for me it didn't crease the door; it just pushed it in a bit. I was able to take the inside door panel off and pop it back out. The result was a fully restored door without the hint of damage. I call that forgiveness. I made a mistake that caused damage, but the damaged item forfeited the induced claim to the point where it was totally renewed to its original condition. The door was very forgiving and lucky for me, so was my friend.

To be fair, forgiveness comes much easier when the

damage is restorable to perfection. When consequence is void and there's nothing to point to and complain about, forgiveness is the path of no resistance. However, when a storm leaves broken branches and shattered lives, then the heart of man is really tested for what its level of forgiveness is. The ultimate test, at times, ends up being the one where we need to forgive the person in the mirror. It seems natural to be harder on ourselves then we are on others but that's when forgiveness can matter the most.

Forgiveness comes naturally to some people. They bend like skinny trees in the wind when life throws a storm their way, naturally bouncing right back into their original position after the storm has past. They are somehow able to pick up the pieces and sweep them into the box of life's trials and lessons where they can remember the pieces, but are protected against any further burden. They have an amazing, God given quality that allows forgiveness to flourish. I'm talking about the quality of grace.

For others, forgiveness is a constant battle because they feel cheated in a way that only retribution, apart from compensation, can resolve. In some cases they want justice; in other cases revenge. Even after retribution and compensation are paid in full, some may carry bitterness around as a token reminder that life wasn't fair to them. It's as if mere recollection isn't good enough; the pain needs to be kept fresh as anti-venom against further harm. Some may even believe that if the pain stops the justice is void, so they bravely carry the pain to honor the victim(s). The problem remains in the fact that where unforgiveness stays, love struggles.

The Math of Forgiveness

True forgiveness is critical for love to be genuine. Without it, the practice of love can be blocked totally or at the least, changed from a conscious good intention to a subconscious, spiteful surrender. Try as we may to hide it, if we don't forgive, an emotional wall is built between us and the ones we are trying to love. Bags of proverbial love can be handed over the wall to an offending party like a disingenuous welcome basket, but they can never be personally delivered with a whole heart because the wall blocks the unforgiving from going all the way in true love. What we end up with is half hearted love that will always disappoint us. It's like trying to wash your car with dirty water. It may appear to be cleaner in the shade but once the light hits it, the dirt stands out.

The Bible teaches us a great deal about forgiveness. In fact it seems from Genesis to Revelations, forgiveness is an underlying, foundational theme throughout all sixty six books. God is very clear about at least three things in his word. First and foremost is that he loves us more than we can ever know or reciprocate. Over and over he shows his love through his providence and guidance in our lives, if we only follow his lead. Second is the unfortunate fact that we all miss the mark we were created to hit. That's the literal translation of sin; to miss the mark. It's not that the mark was designed to be too difficult to hit, it's just that it leaves no room for selfishness and the human condition is incurably infested with selfishness.

The third thing God's very clear about is that he's always ready to fully forgive us of all our shortfalls if only we repent, or literally "turn back" to him and follow him again. This is truly where all our hope lays for an eternal life. We absolutely must believe this. This fact was the main force behind Jesus' ministry; that God loved us so much that he gave his only son, that whoever believes in Him will have eternal life. He's not saying "believe I exist" or "believe I am really God" as much as Jesus is saying "trust that I love you and want to be with you forever, to the point that I will pay all your debt and forgive all your sins if you just believe that I can, and follow me".

When we put God first in our lives, believing in his son is a much easier thing to do. It's when we choose to do it our way (putting us first instead) that we continue to struggle with accepting this gracious gift of forgiveness. Apart from selfishness, it makes absolutely no sense not to believe that Jesus died for our sins. A quick cursory look at the facts is more than enough to get you started.

The fact that Jesus was an actual person in history is indisputable. When we take all the physical, archeological and recorded information into account, we have every reason to believe he is who he says he is. If he isn't the son of God then he was either a raving lunatic or the biggest con artist in history; but the data doesn't support insanity or a con, it supports a Savior. In regards to the resurrection of Jesus; if we were to bring the case to court today, the evidence would be overwhelmingly convincing to the point that it would meet and exceed most precedents for being deemed provable fact.

Please don't believe me; look it up yourself. Do an honest, unbiased assessment of the facts and see where they lead. On the theoretical side, if cause and effect have any scientific merit, what would we make of the countless documented miracles in Jesus name? I'm not talking about the ones you see on TV. I'm talking about the hospital bedside ones that doctors file away without explanation or publicity. I'm talking about the total changes in personality, going from addiction victims or violent criminals to productive community members and humble servants.

There is insurmountable, measurable evidence available to those who wish to seek out the effects of Jesus Christ and the Holy Spirit on the lives of people all over the globe. In this life there are many gray areas and many unanswered questions. With Jesus Christ there are clear answers and a clear direction for our lives; now, and for our lives to come. Accepting his forgiveness and guidance now is critical to our fulfillment in eternity. However, the forgiveness and grace of God isn't only available to bank for an eternal home some day. It has very practical applications for here and now.

Unshackled

If you haven't done so already, I suggest you read the timeless Christian classic, "Pilgrims' Progress" by John Bunyan. (Even better, get the DVD put out by DRC Films, LLC in

2008. It's an excellent modern day visual depiction!) In this timeless parable, a man named Christian, who lives in the City of Destruction, finds himself struggling more and more with the weight of a burden he has strapped to his back that will inevitably lead to the demise of both him and his family. The more he learns of God, the more he understands his sinful nature and the heavier the burden gets.

At one point in the story, Christian comes upon a cross where the power and grace of forgiveness allows the straps of the burden to break and the burden falls away. Once the burden is gone, Christian is free to love God without fear or restraint. He finds a new strength and confidence to carry on his journey to the gates of Heaven and the Eternal City of the Lord.

As theatrical as this story sounds, it's not far off the actual mark of what forgiveness can do for you and I. When we hold back on forgiveness, we sometimes think it's punishing the unforgiven, and once in a while we're right. But each and every time we do we are punishing ourselves and hurting God. Like the burden in the story, an unforgiving heart causes the carrier to be weighed down and stressed. All too often the people we don't forgive have long forgotten what we're clinging to. It can be years before someone finds out that we've been carrying a grudge against them, if they find out at all. In most cases, they don't even remember the offense, and actually pity us when they realize we've been plagued all the while for something they never thought twice about. Here again, sometimes the person we find the hardest to forgive is the one in the mirror.

I had an experience like this not too long ago. I mentioned in an earlier chapter that I had moved to Colorado for a while after breaking off a marriage engagement.I moved out there with my best friend from High School. We shared an apartment together and we both took jobs as electrician apprentices for a local firm. One day at a job site I was asked to move his van so a truck could get by. I was in a rush and not paying close enough attention and I accidentally slammed his van into a parked excavator. Needless to say the excavator didn't budge and showed no sign of the collision. My friends' van was a different story. His right front fender was crunched! It looked terrible but luckily it didn't affect the drivability at all. Since I was broke and stupid, I decided to act like it didn't happen. When he asked me about it I pulled a Peter and denied three times I ever knew the crash.

The next night my friend had the ugly task of bringing to my attention the fact that there was a witness to the whole thing. The witness pointed squarely to me as the guilty party. I stood speechless in my humiliation and shame, as my friend asked me why I lied to him. I had no excuse. I was a coward and a weasel about the crash and broke a trust that I shouldn't have. For years that incident plagued my mind. A few times since it happened I wanted to say I was sorry for the whole thing but I couldn't muster the courage. I wouldn't find the courage for twenty seven years.

My friend, who is with the National Forest Service,

had moved around the country a lot with each promotion he took. One of his most recent locations was Lexington, Kentucky. We were talking on the phone about the new house and he said he planned to finish off his basement and make it into a TV/Game room. I offered to come down and help for a few days in exchange for his old dirt bike. It was an old Suzuki PE 250 we used to ride when we were teenagers. He was more than happy to accept the deal since his wife was very tired of dragging the bike from location to location and it hadn't run in years.

The drive down took about twelve hours. I listened to music and a book on tape to pass the time. After a while I started thinking about the times we had over the years and like a pulled muscle that never quite healed, the stinging pain of the crash came flooding back into my mind. Why was I so stupid then? How could I lie to my best friend like that? And why haven't I ever had the courage to say I was sorry? On the trip down I decided that the first chance I got, I needed to apologize for the way I handled that incident.

I got there around 3:45pm and got settled in. My friend had a daily ritual where he'd walk his dogs around the block and asked me if I'd like to join him. As we walked, the guilt weighed heavily on my heart, as it did so many times before. But this time I was determined to move it up the few inches from my heart and push it out of my mouth.

I felt as humble as I'd ever been when I confessed that I needed to get something off my chest. I asked him to recall the day when I had lied about the crash and admitted that

I never really apologized like I should of; like he deserved. I fought back the lump in my throat and the tears in my eyes as I said I was so sorry for breaking his trust and lying to him; and that I wish I could relive that day and make it right.

My friend looked at me in astonishment. "Are you kidding me? You still think about that?" he said with a slight chuckle. He, in his God given grace, had let that go the day after he confronted me back in Colorado. For 27 years I had his blessing of forgiveness but I didn't have my own. I was carrying this burden all this time, beating myself up for it; all the while he never gave it another thought. It wasn't his fault that I carried this burden all this time. It was my fault! I was the unforgiving one; hurting myself and hurting God. It wasn't until I apologized the way I thought I should that I felt I had the right to lay it down and never again pick it up.

Was I wrong to hold myself accountable? I'd say the answer is no. What I will say is that the Bible is right when it says not to let the sun go down without resolving a conflict. If you stall, you could be carrying the weight of it around for a very long time. Needless to say I breathed a lot easier for the rest of the week and was very glad that I got that behind me so soon in the visit.

Is there something that you carry with you day after day? Has the day after day turned into year after year? Isn't it time for you to forgive, whether it be someone who has done you wrong or yourself for something you regret doing?

Don't let the sun go down again before you take care of it. Do you need forgiveness? If you need to confess something then do it; don't wait! If there's no opportunity to confess it to the person you hurt, then confess it to God. He already knows about it and has been waiting for you to talk to him. Ask for forgiveness and then accept the forgiveness. There is genuine peace in forgiveness; the kind of peace we need to be healthy. We were never designed to carry the burden that holding a grudge creates.

The Wonder of Grace

There is nothing in all the human experience that God has not forgiven already. He is painfully aware of everything we do to each other down here on Earth. There never was, is, or will ever be someone who has the right to say to God "but Lord, you don't know what I've done". He's seen it all, and still he loves and forgives us.

Understand; for every sin, large or small, there is an accounting. That's just the way it works. Justice has to be paid. There's no sin ever committed that doesn't demand payment. That's why death is here. Death is the penalty. Jesus knew this all too well. The religious leaders of his day questioned his authority to forgive sins, and in their defense, rightfully so. They also knew that Gods' justice was true and that every sin carried a penalty. What they didn't know was that God's love was greater than anyone's shortfalls. His love went to the extent of exacting payment for all sin from his only son who himself, freely gave his life in exchange for the lives of you and I. The religious leaders of his day had no idea they were questioning the very one who already signed up to pay the price.

No matter how terrible an offense, God's grace is more terrific. No matter how bad we think we are, Gods' goodness can still redeem us. As deep into the darkness we may stray, the light of God can still show us the way back, if we only seek it out. He doesn't care how bad you were or how many times you denied him in the past. If you turned your back on him a thousand times, he will still be there waiting for you to turn back to him.

While we have breath in our lungs it's not too late. Although he'd prefer a life of loving service, he'll always accept a deathbed confession. If only you could be sure you were going to die in bed with a few minutes to dwell on things, right? The risky reality is that you need to be a sincere believer and that takes time for the human heart to absorb. If meaningless words were all we'd need then many more of us could be saved. God knows your heart and he knows your motives. He wants your friendship, not your fear. He wants to be first in your life, not a last resort.

My pastor frequently mentions in his sermons that now is the acceptable time to believe. Today is the day to take your faith seriously; not tomorrow because there's no guarantee you'll live to see it. And today is the day to forgive others so that you can accept Gods' forgiveness. The Lords' Prayer provides for us a rule to live by when it says "...and forgive us our sins, as we forgive those who've sinned against us". What if this is a mathematical formula that's built into the laws of love? What if we die and go before God, and he says that he wanted and waited to forgive us, but couldn't because we never forgave others? What if the rule is that we can't accept forgiveness without giving it first? By holding back forgiveness we would be condemning ourselves.

Don't die holding a grudge or you may have to carry it though all eternity. Don't live another day without getting rid of it. You don't need it. Give it to God and let him deal with it, because he promises he will. Trade it in for the grace and love of God and I promise you that you will have a happier, healthier life.

In our lives we will experience offenses and we will certainly offend others. We'll endure unjust pain and inflict unjust pain upon others. As we drift through this earthly experience, it's inevitable. But God in his mercy has provided a way for us to love despite these conflicts to peace. He gives us his forgiveness and he also gives us hearts equipped to share that forgiveness with others.

God has given each of us millions of dollars worth of forgiveness and asks us to spend a few hundred of it on each other. We can do this if we take our eyes off our pain and focus on his love. It seems easier said then done but it's not impossible, and it's easier than we tend to make it. If you struggle to forgive, ask God for help. Speak to someone about it. Don't let it eat you up. Life is too short and your purpose here is too important to be sidelined by an unforgiving heart.

Keep Your Eye on the Goal

"...for God created us for incorruption, and made us in the image of his own eternity."
King Solomom

In his book "A Case for Faith", Lee Strobel tells a small story that demonstrates a big lesson. He shares how he sat, somewhat stressed out, watching his young daughter thread her very first needle. Time and again she would prick her finger. With each misalignment, Lee could almost feel the needle jab into his own finger. He fought the temptation to break in and do it for her and save her little digits the pain. Any father would want to help, but he valued the lesson she was learning too much to interfere. To his credit, he held back, hidden from sight as he watched her many attempts. He witnessed the stinging pain in her eyes as she repeatedly poked herself. He also witnessed her resolve overcome her fear of the pain. Then finally, she succeeded. She yelled out in triumph, "Daddy, look what I did!" In an instant, all the pain she suffered was forgotten; dissipating into the atmosphere of victory.

This is just one of a billion such success stories we are blessed to witness daily. With each one there are two truths to appreciate. The first is that when pursuing a dream or goal, we all suffer the consequences of the work it takes to achieve them. Nothing of real worth ever comes easy; there's always a price to pay. It may sound strange but I think we should embrace our cost as a blessing.

When done honestly, hard work builds strong character. The meat of our pride is in recognizing the total effort it took to accomplish something. An item hard earned always brings more satisfaction then an item handed to you without cost. Who of us, that has successfully built something praiseworthy, no longer feels the pride when we see it again? It's an outstanding feeling when someone says "Wow, that's nice!" and you can say "I did that!"

The second reality is the importance of keeping our eyes on the goal. As we walk through life there are surely times when it helps to look down at the ground, carefully watching our steps as we go. However, throughout the whole journey, it is better to keep your head up and eyes forward as much as you can, so that you never lose sight of your final destination.

Eternal Hope

I read a story once about a woman who attempted to swim the English Channel. Although she started strong, the weather changed and the waves were against her. She struggled during the last part of the journey and, in the late of the night, totally exhausted, she finally gave up. Her follow boat anchored for a bit and pulled her on board.

The team tried to comfort her as she sat on deck in terrible disappointment. It was a long cold night and they could only imagine how badly she felt about her failure to finish. "It's so dark, I couldn't see anything" she said as she sat, clutching the blanket around her. She rested there a while; occasionally wiping the tears from her cheeks. Just then the sun began to rise and in the distance she started to see something. It was land. As if adding insult to injury, the reality of it sank in. She had given up not half a mile from the shore. After struggling in the water for over sixteen hours it was the darkness that defeated her. She knew in her heart that, had she been able to see the land, she would have finished.

Does this sound painfully familiar? Do you have a similar story to tell? Have you ever attempted something big, only to succumb to waves crashing against you in the darkness? So many unforeseen problems seem to crop up; every one of them blocking your view of the goal you set out for.

Sometimes we get so bogged down by life's distractions and challenges that we forget what we're living for. An all too common example is when we have a job to support our family, only to have the job so consume us that we leave little or no time for family at all. It's as if we set out on a journey, clearly seeing our destination, but then get to a point in the road where we have no idea where we are. We don't know how we got there and we've forgotten what our destination was to begin with. All the smoke and mirrors of this world distract and confuse us and leave us feeling lost.

For Christians, our goal and final destination is eternal life with God and with those we love. Eternity, as invisible as it seems, is something that we all need to keep our emotional and spiritual eyes on. Heaven is our home. Everything we are doing here on Earth should be predicated on the goal of staying on the right path; the path that brings us home to be with the author of love and creator of our souls.

Whenever we take time to think about eternity with God and the ones we love, who we believe are in Heaven now, it is by no means a small thing. I often encounter people who brush it off as some light hearted subject, like a movie they plan to see some day if they ever get the time. For those of us who truly believe in God and what he says in his word, their apathy is a very disturbing concern. Too many people presume that if they can't see it or prove it's there, they'll settle on letting the winds of fate carry them where it will, if anywhere at all; and until the time comes, they just won't worry about it. After all, this life has enough to deal with without worrying about the next, right? The truth is they couldn't be more wrong!

When we give way to this mindset, we miss the whole point of this life. We're not here to entertain ourselves, conquer others or blindly swim through swamps of relativism. This is a finite period of time we have to point ourselves in the right direction before shooting off into all eternity. Left by ourselves we are blindly shooting in the dark, not knowing where the target is. That's exactly what the enemy wants us to do. Satan knows that if he can distract us long enough, we'll die without God in our lives and then he can rule over us throughout all eternity like a sadistic kid with a live bug collection.

Jesus tells us in John 16:33,

> "I have told you these things, so that in me you may have peace. In this world you will have trouble. But take heart! I have overcome the world."

Did you catch that first part? Jesus himself told us "these things" so that we could have peace. Being apathetic and uninformed about what your long term future holds will ***not*** bring peace. On the contrary, apathy of this sort breeds aimlessness. Aimlessness breeds hopelessness and that leads to nowhere! We need to be sure of exactly where we're going, and in this passage Jesus is helping us to find it.

Just before this, in verse 32, Jesus warned his disciples that trouble will come and they will scatter and leave him alone. Yet he assures them that he won't be alone because his father will be with him. He is saying, in essence, that with God we are never really alone and that if he is connected with his father and we stay connected with him, we can count on the peace that only comes from God. Then in verse 33 he shares this truth with them so that in him they can understand and have peace about it.

In these verses, Jesus gives us a glimpse, a hint of what the path to eternity is all about. And although he was speaking to his disciples, he also speaks to us today. What Jesus is saying is that he knows this world has troubles. He implies that we will make the mistake of forgetting him from time to time as we scatter from the fears of this world. But if we return and put our trust and faith in him, he will lead us through this world so that we can reach the next world in peace.

Immediately following this, in chapter 17, Jesus then prays to his Father in Heaven that through the glory of God, all who believe in Jesus may have eternal life with him. That's the goal for us. We will no doubt endure suffering in this world, especially if we confess belief in Jesus. But he promises us peace during this relatively brief earthly trial and an eternity of love with Him and the Father.

A Familiar Voice

This world, in comparison to what God designed it to be, is a dark and confusing place. Yes, there are many beautiful aspects of creation and of the humanity that rules over it, but there are also many perversions and corruptions that have worked their stains into the fabric of our physical world.

Beginning with a violent birth process, we come out screaming; cold and dirty, covered in material you'd never touch if given the option. We go through life being prodded by hunger and thirst. We labor for things we need to survive before we labor for things we enjoy. We all have a deep seeded understanding and appreciation for the truth that it's better to be loved than to not be loved, yet we struggle to both give and receive love.

On the average we instinctively cling to, and promote what is good, and shy away from what is evil. Our hearts are blessed by stories of compassion and mercy, even as immoral sex and senseless violence carry our entertainment industry. Why are we so ethically and morally bipolar? We have been created in the image of God, yet as generations pass, we drift farther and farther to the left as we listen to the voices of relative reason saying there is no God, there is no absolute right or wrong; there is no underlying purpose for our lives. We are hopeless!

Friedrich Nietzsche, a famous, late 19th century philosopher and critic of Christianity has two very interesting quotes regarding the subject of hope:

> "In reality, hope is the worst of all evils, because it prolongs man's torments." ...yet he also said; "Strong hope is a much greater stimulant of life than any realized joy could be."

Nietzsche's quotes on hope, as different as they seem, both point to a solid truth, which is that hope is a powerful force. If Nietzsche didn't believe in the idea of his soul being eternal, then these quotes make perfect sense. Hope does give us strength when there is nothing else to draw from. Yet if when we die, we end, mind body and soul; then hope is evil because it mocks us by giving us power in a powerless situation. We are like children at a store front, left staring through the glass at the toy we long for, yet would never enjoy playing with. Nietzsche's hope hangs like a key just out of reach, to a prison cell we're trapped in while the hourglass empties before our eyes. What a sad state to live in.

Yes, at times this world is truly a dark and confusing place indeed! But don't give up! There's another voice there; a voice older than the stars in the night sky. It surpasses all the false wisdom of this world. It's the voice of the one who loves you the most. It's the voice of your creator, the Prince of Peace. He wants always to remind you of your goal; a true and loving relationship with him, and with all the others he has created who choose to follow him. Many of them you already know and love; some you have yet to meet.

Putting aside the unimaginable joy we will experience in meeting our creator face to face, as we feel every bit of our faith and hope validated in His affirming love; and setting aside the peace and security we will feel as Jesus smiles on us as he welcomes us home; once our hearts begin to recover from that enormous wave of happiness, we will still be in the middle of the grandest reunion we will ever have!

You'll meet ancestors that have kept the faith for generations in Heaven as they watched your family's lives down here on earth unfold. You will meet members of your very own bloodline reaching back hundreds and thousands of years. You'll meet heroes of the past going all the way back to Adam and Eve. They are people that you've read about, studied, learned from and have been inspired by. Perhaps one of the biggest surprises will be in learning who the real heroes are as judged by God. Who's to say that your Great Great Grandmother won't beat out George Washington?

You'll be pleasantly surprised to see that all the good deeds you've done here on Earth, forgotten and unnoticed in this life, will be celebrated in Heaven, as you meet those you've touched by your generosity and compassion. You will come to realize that not one good or loving thing you do on Earth is ever wasted. It all counts towards the glory of God!

As exciting as this life can be when we walk with God, the next will be a never ending wonder. We will see so many things hidden from our earthly eyes. All your questions will be answered and a whole new learning will bring endless questions and answers as you experience eternity in all its boundless beauty. With death no longer a reality (which is mind blowing enough) you will be able to see more clearly, what your true purpose for eternal existence is. It's well worth your while to take time from your stressful life now and dream a bit about the excitingly peaceful life to come, if you choose to follow God.

Through a variety of venues God points us to eternity and to the incorruptible treasures that await those who follow him. With earthly experiences, God is ever providing opportunities for us to correct our course so that we head in the right direction.

Cynics are quick to discredit God by voicing examples of this world's cruelty. If God is love, then why wasn't he there for the many victims of violence and war? How can we find God in the injustice of genocide? Why aren't the innocent protected? These are valid questions asked through the very real pain of burdened hearts. The answer is in the fact that, believe it or not, God was, is and will always be here. The answer is also posed back to us by this very same God. Why aren't ***we*** there for the widow, the orphan or victims of violence and war? More to the point; why are ***we*** causing all this pain and suffering in the world? God has demonstrated nothing but goodness and righteousness as a model for us and still we ignore him and follow our own selfish, self destructive model instead.

One could argue the case for natural disasters and indiscriminant disease taking perfectly innocent lives. Where is God in that? Why does he allow such things? Yet in asking these questions, the assumptions are that, first; God planned it to be this way, and second; God isn't feeling any of the pain we're feeling. In both cases we'd be wrong to assume this.

In the first case, the creation was never meant to be so violent. It was Man's decision to walk away from God that cursed the creation; not God. And his word promises that some day the creation will be fully restored to its original design; a world of peace and full providence; one without pain or disease or disaster.

The second assumption that God doesn't feel our pain

couldn't be more wrong. On the contrary, because of his deep love for us, He feels the pain more then we do. His love is so deep and his pain is so intense that the better alternative was for him to allow his one and only son to suffer a horrible torture and death, so that our history won't end in the hopelessness of it all. It's precisely because of his pain that we will ultimately be healed. All we need to do is believe in him.

God is love. Whether we choose to acknowledge it or not, we are all living in a world infused with love. Unfortunately, because of evil, the world is also infused with hate and corruption. With our own free will, we as a species have strayed so far from God's plan that we no longer recognize the call of choosing love to practice. As we focus on this world and stray from God's plan, our hearts seem to have forgotten why we were created. In our self centered, worldly neglect of God's plan, we come to face one of the greatest dangers imaginable, which is becoming ignorant of the reality of eternity.

Whatever this life force is that sustains us in this physical world, it is energy that transfers somewhere when our physical bodies give out. Atheists hope for their best case scenario of just ending. No life after life, no ongoing recollection. If they are right then ultimately everything we do or experience here is pointless. If they are correct then love itself is a foolish waste of time as it seems to only bring trials and pain in the world we live in.

But what if they are wrong? What if they die physically

but remain in spirit? This misdirection places them at risk of entering eternity without the love that surrounds them now. That's a very scary thought! If it doesn't scare you then you don't fully understand what real love produces.

Light, warmth, friendship, relationships, laughter, health; all these are a product of love. Without any of them and many other positive things that are created in love, eternity will be a terrible place to be. In fact, an eternity devoid of all these positive attributes is the very definition of Hell. The real truth is that even at its worst, this world is still a place where God is. His love is evident in all the goodness we experience. As dark as it gets, we can still choose to bring light into the world for others to see and hope in.

The story of Corrie ten Boom is a beautiful example of how we can choose to love despite the darkness all around us. In her true life story, "The Hiding Place", this innocent young lady is victimized by the ugliness of the Holocaust. Inspired by her sisters' unwavering faith in God, Corrie learned to find love in the darkest parts of her human experience. Through everything she endured, she kept her focus on God's love, sharing it whenever she could, even with her captors. If people like Corrie ten Boom, with all her horrifying experiences in a Nazi concentration camp, can keep her focus on the love of God, then so can we.

Real love is eternal. God wants more than anything to love us and teach us how to love one another. If we turn to him and seek his face, we will find him and find our purpose for this life as well as the next. If I'm right in my belief that we're all created, first and foremost to love God and love one another, then it makes perfect sense that eternity with him (and those who follow him) is the destination this life is leading to. In light of that, we should all help each other as much as we possibly can to seek Gods' direction as we learn to love.

Doing to the Least of These

"How wonderful it is that nobody need wait a single moment before starting to improve the world."
Anne Frank

There was a TV commercial that used to play on Sunday mornings a few years ago. I can't recall who the sponsor was but I'll never forget its message. It was brief as most commercials are and it centered on the morning rituals of two teenage girls. Both girls got up at the same time every morning before school. They were both average American teens; average in size and looks and both seemed to be healthy. They could easily be the girls living on your street in your home town.

As the camera flashed between their two simultaneous lives it began to reveal the individual focus each girl nurtured in the way their lives were going. The first girl would be showered and dressed and on the road in no time. The second would take her time, studying herself in the early morning mirror. The first girl pulls into a parking lot and enters a building. The second girl begins sifting through possible designer outfit combinations. The first is greeted by a group of small children who are bubbling over with enthusiasm as they once again welcome their mentor and hero. The second girl hears her mother yelling up to her to get going or she'll be late. She yells back with indifferent acknowledgement as she carefully applies another coat of toenail polish.

The first girl is seen finishing up a story time session as she puts her book down and hugs all her little friends before leaving for school. Although sad that she has to leave, you can see in them the energetic peace that she leaves their tender hearts with. She smiles a big smile as she waves goodbye and promises to be back soon. They light up at the thought of her return. She hops back into her car and drives away. The camera skips to her destination where she pulls up to the home of the second girl who is just coming out of her house. The second girl gets in the front seat. The commercial comes to a simple end as they exchange "good mornings" and begin the drive to school.

Even with the television volume all the way off you'd hear the message of that commercial loud and clear. Some of us seem content focusing mainly on the three foot by three foot area affectionately known as our personal space. How do I look? How do I feel? What do I need? What do

I want? These are natural questions, but at their core, what is the nature of them?

Rethinking Comfort

From the moment we leave the womb our first and foremost concern is our comfort. At the most basic level of life we need that built-in mechanism to survive; that's why we cry right away. Sure, we can blame the initial few seconds on the doctor if he or she whacks our backsides to activate our lungs, but what about the following seconds, minutes, days and years? It's understandable if an infant is self-centered and needy but are we supposed to stay there as we grow? At what point in our lives does this behavior convert from a basic instinct of survival to a self serving, self satisfying pursuit of being comfortable?

Don't get me wrong, there's nothing wrong with living a comfortable life. God himself promotes this concept right from the beginning in the book of Genesis. He created the Garden of Eden; a magnificent place filled with all types of amazing life forms, abundant, self replenishing food sources and an endless supply of cool, fresh water. The climate of the environment was such that man had no need of clothing to protect himself from nature's elements. He would never freeze in winter or be burned by the suns' heat. In addition to providing for these fundamental needs, the garden was also designed to provide man with ample entertainment and exercise.

In Genesis 2:15 God says; "The Lord God took the man

and put him in the Garden of Eden to work it and take care of it." God knew that mankind would be happiest when being productive. As you can imagine, a garden designed by God would provide mankind with a perpetual harvest to work with. And although there was plenty to do in the garden, nothing in it produced stress or anxiety; that is, at least until Satan showed up!

There's absolutely no doubt about it; Gods' design for us was, is and will always be a plan of comfort and blessing. That doesn't mean we have the right to lazily lounge around like the pathetic state of "human" existence depicted in the Pixar movie "Wall-E"; ever floating in recliner chairs while robots tend to our every need. God knows we want more than that. God also knows that, as he feels blessed loving and providing for our needs, we also will feel blessed loving and helping each other.

I think that God had this blessing in mind when he created Eve. I like to think that he did it for two main reasons. The first is obvious because God explained it in Genesis, chapter 2:18 when he said: "It is not good for the man to be alone. I will make a helper suitable for him." He knows we need others in our lives to help us. No one wants to be alone! But I also like to think there's a secret code for Adam in the word "helper". I wonder if the original text actually spelled it this way: HELP-HER. Alright, I'll admit that's a fanciful stretch of my own imagination, but I'll use it to make a point that we, as husbands, don't consider as much as we should; which is that maybe we were created to serve our wives at least as much as they were created to serve us.

Serving Each Other

What if God created marriage for us to learn and grow in love through the practice of helping each other? Marriage is the perfect platform to build on when it comes to service to others because it begins at a "nuclear" level. By that I mean a man and a woman have different strengths and weaknesses that help pull them together in love; much like the natural forces found in the atom. As husband and wife are brought into a bond, they form the basic nuclear family, and through their love expand that with children. Throughout each step in this process, each individual part learns to both serve and be served by the others, and so naturally fulfill the commandment to love one another.

I remember the first time I attended a Promise Keepers Conference back in 1996. It was at the Carrier Dome in Syracuse, New York. In case you're not familiar with "PK", it is an organization that was created to help men become the spiritual leaders of integrity that God intended them to be. Whether our role in the world would be husband, father, son or brother, we desperately need to come to Christ and follow him so that through his love and guidance, we can help lead our families the way they want and need us to.

I remember one speaker in particular. His name was Pastor Joseph Garlington. He shared a mindset with the crowd that I'm ashamed to say, until he mentioned it, I'd never thought of its perspective on a marriage. He said,

"Gentlemen, as Christians it is our jobs to out-serve our wives."

Out-serve our wives? Is he crazy? What's that supposed to mean? I was running the comparisons through my mind. I work full time and she works part time. I work overtime and she gets to take the kids to their games and hang out with them. I help cook, sometimes. I help clean, sometimes. She doesn't want me touching the laundry! Is that my fault?

As he told his story it was clear that he had a passion to serve his wife and family. It was like a mission to him. He shared how he and his wife were getting ready for work one morning and he wasn't sure which dress she wanted to wear so he ironed 2 of them and hung them up so she'd see them when she came out of the bathroom. He told her he wasn't sure what she'd want to wear so he ironed two dresses to give her a choice. She was so moved that she began to cry with humbled joy over how her husband was so diligent to take care of her. When she was out of view and ear shot, he pulled his fist in to his side and loudly whispered to himself. "YES!" He said to us with comical pride, "I made her cry! It was beautiful!"

We all laughed at the thought of his pride in making her cry, but after the crowd settled down again, he once again got serious with us. He repeated his message; "Men, make it your mission to out-serve your wives!"

Of all the messages I've heard at the various conferences I've been to over the years, I think that one message spoke to my heart the most. For me to say that I love my neighbor as myself, I need make sure that I start with the closest human neighbors I have, namely, my wife and children. I believe in the equality of men and women in many respects but I also recognize the distinct differences between us. I believe that God designed us to be different in ways that lend to our practice of loving and serving each other in specific ways.

I, for one, enjoy loving my wife through out-serving her. We often lightly banter back and forth about who loves who more and she pretty much always forfeits the edging by saying "You do love me more!" Although I know she loves me with all her heart and proves her love and devotion daily, I take pride in the fact that she still says that I love her more. As long as I live and am physically able, I will fight to keep that precious trophy by out-serving her.

I don't mean to sound sexist or chauvinistic but I feel that God has called on us men to be the spiritual leaders of our families. That doesn't make us any better or more powerful but it does make us more accountable. Of all the responsibilities we have as men, this one has got to be the most important, for on our shoulders are the souls of many who would come after us in life. We need to be deliberate in the legacy we leave them.

Selfless Love

Some say that you can't really begin to love others until you truly love yourself first. I suppose there's some truth in that statement, but I also believe that no matter how we feel about ourselves, we can still successfully love others. When we begin to shift our concerns away from our needs and towards the needs of others, we begin to feel the natural blessings of service. It's a beautiful, fulfilling experience that rests deep down into our souls as we practice selfless acts. In doing so we promote self confidence and self esteem which naturally lend to the love we need for ourselves. God designed this type of service to enrich our lives as we exercise the commandment to love one another.

There's no better or more natural expression of selfless love than that of a parent. From the moment the baby enters the world, Mom and Dad are in constant motion and commotion over the safety, security and comfort of their child. A friend of mine once put it this way as we discussed fatherhood with a new Dad; he said "It's all about sacrifice!" We take our pre-parental life as we know it and store it in a shoebox and stick it in our closet for the eighteen to however many years it takes to raise our children to full independence. That may be exaggerating a bit but it sure seems that way at times. And as much as we may complain about it, we wouldn't want to change it. Why wouldn't we? Because of the many, many blessings we've received as we sacrificed our lives for sake of theirs.

Of coarse this parental love isn't reserved only for those who can have children. On the contrary, there are Step-Parents, Foster Parents, Adoptive Parents, Big Brothers and Big Sisters, Aunts and Uncles (blood tied or otherwise) that give every bit as much for the welfare of our young ones (and maybe not so young ones) every day. Choose to see it however you will but I believe it's nothing short of the love of God working through the hearts of those who are open to it.

As God is our Parent who loves us and is forever reaching out to us with guidance and providence, so too are the many people that have been there for you and I throughout our lives, guiding us on our paths and providing for our needs. And in turn, we too with open hearts reach out to others both young and old in a natural effort to share the love and concern that has been afforded us. But it all has to begin when we make the decision to divert our eyes from the mirrored image of ourselves and instead peer out the windows of need that seem to be on every wall of our lives.

You may have heard this positive phrase used as a replacement for the negative thought of being surrounded by needs and problems; it's called "challenges and opportunities!" No one can deny that there's an over abundance of need in the world, but the up side to that is there's also endless opportunities for every type of skill and ability. For every person physically or mentally inhibited from helping others, there are a million people available to help them. And even though those millions of people have needs as well, each of them can use what they have to help each other.

We all have something to give. We all have more ability then we realize. No matter how broke or broken we feel, we still have the capacity to give of ourselves to make the world a better place for others, even if it's a small amount. Every act of kindness counts. Every positive word of encouragement, every helping hand, every nickel in the plate, every prayer we offer up on behalf of others; every bit of it is needed by someone and appreciated by God.

There's a slapstick joke that goes; a man walks up to another man and complains that he has a headache. The second man then kicks him square in the shin. The first man lets go of his head and starts rubbing his leg and screams, "what did you go and do that for?" The second man says, "Hey, it made you forget about your headache didn't it?" The funny thing is that this logic makes sense. We tend to always concentrate on the most painful parts! The application here is that we need to take our eyes off our headaches and focus on the bigger pains in the lives of others so we can be there to comfort them. When we do we'll find that we tend to forget we ever had a headache.

Small Groups

I was talking with a Pastor at a party once and he asked me if I had ever heard of the concept of small groups. At first I thought it was a trick question but them he explained. He said the way he understood it, it's not big churches with thousands of members that God prefers, although he can certainly use them; it's the small groups that are intentionally formed right in the community that work most efficiently.

The concept intrigued me but it took a deeper explanation

of the model for me to really grasp what he was getting at. As he posed examples I couldn't help but think this is what life used to be like before our culture drifted into the personally independent lifestyle we practice today.

Imagine you go to the neighbor on your left and on your right and introduce yourself, share your skills and abilities and offer them help if they need. You also ask them if they'd like to join you for half an hour or so once or twice a week to worship at your house. The worship time could include Bible study, prayer and praise. They accept and before you know it, you begin to build solid relationships with those closest to you on your street. As you continue to meet, you each share your different talents with each other, not out of personal gain but in the spirit of the original church where people brought all they had and shared it with each other in promotion of love. Soon you each begin to reach out to those houses on the outside of this little circle, adding a few more people. Before you know it, you have a handful more sharing support, talents and worship.

As time goes on, your hearts are woven together in friendship as you share each others' burdens and trials as well as celebrate each others accomplishments and successes. And as beautiful a thing that is, the best part is that as a small group you're able to dive deeper into worship, helping each other draw much closer to God than would ever be possible in a larger group setting.

Once or twice a month you could carpool as a group to the local house of worship to join with other people in the greater community. There you will still have the broader church service experience where you enjoy the excitement of the hundreds or thousands, with a choir and a band and a trained Pastor or Priest that would connect you with the churches greater missions and activities.

The point of the small group model is that it decreases the separation between ourselves and those around us. We live in a fiercely independent culture that doesn't lend itself to the style of community that God originally intended. We were meant to be more involved with each others lives than we are now. I'm not saying we need to forfeit all privacy because much like Jesus practiced; it's healthy to get away from the crowds to a private place for rest and solitude. However there are great benefits to every individual as they take a more active role in practicing small group community.

One obvious benefit of this model is that it makes good use of diversity. Maybe I can't cook but I trim a mean hedge. So I trim your hedge and you make me dinner. That's a very simple example, but with a little imagination you can begin to see that hiring contractors you don't know at a price you'd rather not pay could become a thing of the past. Sharing talents and skills is what keeps the cost of managing many a church property down year after year. The same benefits could be gained in smaller community group settings.

Another benefit of the small group is that it inherently reduces temptations in our lives. Things we may struggle with on our own are much easier to fight against when we have friends that are close, not only in relationship but also in physical location; like right next door!

Ecclesiastes 4:12 says "Though one may be overpowered, two can defend themselves. A cord of three strands is not quickly broken". We need others who we can trust to stand by us if we need; someone who can hold us accountable. Today's culture is rife with temptations and traps that we are too easily captured by. We need others in our lives that will help us out of the pits we fall into.

One of the biggest benefits I can think of for starting or participating in a small group setting is that it greatly increases our ability to fulfill the second part of the greatest commandment. When we put God first in our lives, he is truly overjoyed; but that's only half of it. We still need to love our neighbors as we love ourselves. Many of us have the up and down thing going well. We reach up to God and feel his love reach down to us. But when it comes to the side to side part, we struggle to reach to our left and right where all the people are. I need to confess that I am as guilty of this as anyone! We come up with all kinds of creative excuses why we withhold love from others, but the truth is we need to do a much better job at sharing what God freely gives us.

The Practice of Service

Loving one another, as a general idea, may seem a bit abstract but when you apply the practical applications of service, it begins to take real root. As we practice serving others, our capacity for love grows, and a yearning to serve is cultivated in the garden of our hearts. Along with that comes the increase of our gratitude for those who serve us. We gain a deeper appreciation for the help we get when we realize the effort it takes to help others.

Serving others comes naturally for some but takes deliberate focus for others. Not everyone is born with a servant's heart. For those who are more accustomed to being served, it's an unnatural feeling at first. However, I truly believe that God has implanted every one of us with the potential to serve others in some way. I also believe that God honors those who fight their self serving instincts and find ways to serve, even against their natural inclinations. Make no mistake; God's plan is that we all cultivate servant hearts. Jesus was very clear about this when he expressed his teaching through the washing of his disciples' feet. His point was that if he, their teacher and master views service as crucial to love, then they too must also serve each other and build on his example.

When I stop to think about all that God has done for me in my life, I am amazed beyond belief. His providence and his grace are endless and inescapable when we open ourselves up to a real relationship with him. He wants more than ever to love us and to teach us to love one another, and a big part of that is realized in service to one another. Remember; love isn't a feeling. It isn't a noun. Love is a verb. It is action. It is doing; and that for others, as much, if not more than for ourselves.

God bless those who give their life to the service of

others. May we all be inspired to heed the call and add to their efforts. Whenever we do, even the smallest amount, it is counted as righteousness in the obedience of God. John put it simply in his first book, chapter 4, verse 12 when he said that "No one has ever seen God; but if we love one another, God lives in us and his love is made complete in us." To serve others is to love others. As we do, we bring God closer to them and we bring ourselves closer to God. And closer to God is the absolute best place we could ever be!

Escaping Our Comfort Zone

"It is not because things are difficult that we do not dare, it is because we do not dare that they are difficult."
Seneca

There is a Chinese proverb that states "A man grows most tired while standing still." I can relate to that. I've had to perform jobs that required standing in the same spot for hours, covering some mind numbing task. If there was an Algebraic equation for it, it would state; NC = NE, or No Challenge = No Excitement.

We were designed to exercise our minds and bodies; to explore and create, to challenge and to conquer. Of coarse I'm not talking about people conquering other people. I am talking about people overcoming fears and achieving goals that at first seem too daunting to take on. I'm talking about ideas and ideals too big to hold back, save the lack of human determination, intervention and forward action.

What would Mount Rushmore mean to America today if South Dakota state historian Doane Robinson and master stone carver Gutzon Borglum had never gotten together with a dream of reshaping the southeast face of that mountain? A lot of words come to mind when thinking about all the planning and hard work behind that monumental undertaking, but "comfortable" is definitely not one of them.

The monuments' face of Thomas Jefferson was dedicated in 1936. President Franklin Roosevelt attended the dedication. He hadn't planned to speak but was so inspired by what he saw, he shared the following;

> "...I had seen the photographs, I had seen the drawings, and I had talked with those who are responsible for this great work, and yet I had no conception, until about ten minutes ago, not only of its magnitude, but also its permanent beauty and importance.
>
> ...I think that we can perhaps meditate on those Americans of 10,000 years from now...meditate and wonder what our descendants - and I think they will still be here - will think about us. Let us hope... that they will believe we have honestly striven every day and generation to preserve a decent land to live in and a decent form of government to operate under."

Although we've only cycled through roughly three generations since that impromptu speech, how would you say we fare? When we look out across today's cultural horizon, does the word "decent" stand out as a leading trait? Let me ask that in a different way. If you had to pick one of two words to describe our culture, would you pick a) decent, or b) comfortable? This may seem to be a loaded question and one could argue that either answer is relative. Yet I would venture to guess that more people would have to pick option b).

In the previous chapter I discussed our natural instinct to pursue comfort in our lives. Comfort isn't a bad thing and it's certainly not a sin to pursue it, unless being comfortable becomes your life's goal. Anything that we place as a priority over our relationship with God will become, as Jesus so aptly put it, "a stumbling block". Whatever it is, it will eventually cause us to trip and fall, away from God. However, when we put God first, He promises to add all things, comfort included, to our lives in a way we would never achieve on our own.

The irony here is that when we put God first in our lives he drives us out of our comfort zone and into our life's mission and purpose. Again, this doesn't mean we say goodbye to all comfort, but it does mean that we don't "live" there every waking moment. The important thing to always remember is the reality that we are eternal beings and not just physical beings. In the real scheme of things, being a child of God for eternity is infinitely more comfortable then living your entire earthly life as a pampered and protected prince or princess without God in your life.

God has specific jobs for every one of us and, more times then not, it involves putting others first and ourselves last. But when we serve others and help others; when we allow God to stretch our hearts and minds and work our muscles to the benefit of others for his name sake, we grow stronger. Anyone who does a hundred stomach crunches or more at a clip will attest to the fact that comfort and work don't always come in pairs. It's the same thing with the work of God. It may at times be painful, - but it's a good pain!

The Impact of Fear

So how does leaving our comfort zone relate to learning to love? I believe the answer to that is hidden in another question which is; what keeps us fenced into a small, tightly controlled area from which we share our love from? The answer to that question is fear! We are afraid to open up our hearts and lives to others because when we do we get hurt.

First John chapter 4:18 sheds some light on how fear can block our ability to love. It says this:

> "There is no fear in love. But perfect love drives out fear, because fear has to do with punishment. The one who fears is not made perfect in love."

If this is true then it stands to reason that as long as we harbor fears about opening up and loving others, we won't be able to love as God wants and needs us to.

John links fear to punishment and punishment is something nobody likes. Merriam-Webster's Dictionary defines punishment this way; "suffering, pain, or loss that serves as retribution; severe, rough, or disastrous treatment." That doesn't sound comfortable at all, yet it seems to be where many of us inadvertently like to hang our hats; in the company of fear!

One of my all time favorite Female Christian artists is Nicole Nordeman. She's a master lyricist and she wrote a song entitled "Brave" which beautifully expresses the point I'd like to make. Here's how she puts it;

> The gate is wide
> The road is paved in moderation
> The crowd is kind and quick to pull you in
> Welcome to the middle ground
> You're safe and sound and
> Until now it's where I've been
>
> 'Cause it's been fear that ties me down to everything
> But it's been love, your love that cuts the strings.

Now truth be told, I believe that the real inspiration for this song was her beloved little boy but it doesn't take a stretch to see God's message in these lyrics.

In Matthew 7:13-14, Jesus taught those following him a truth about survival. He said;

> ""Enter through the narrow gate. For wide is the gate and broad is the road that leads to destruction, and many enter through it. But small is the gate and narrow the road that leads to life and only a few find it."

These verses are speaking of salvation but I think we can read even more into them in that they imply that; easy is the way the world wants us to go. Our self serving culture would have us pursue comfortable moderation over the painful risk of love because it takes less work and appears much safer. But Jesus says a life of real love is entered through a small gate and provides a narrow road to follow.

A small gate isn't found by accident. Anyone wanting to find it needs to be deliberate about looking for it. By deliberate I mean the seeker has to mindfully push aside the worlds' views of love and look for the hidden gates and paths that God has provided for us. They are there to be sure but they don't flash all the trappings and false promises that worldly paths post.

To enter a small gate, we would have to shrink a bit. I'm not saying that we'd need to physically shrink. What I am saying is that we'd have to crouch, or bring ourselves lower then we normally are. In other words, we'd need to humble ourselves. The same idea applies to the narrow path. Have you ever been hiking and come upon a section of a path that was overgrown? Have you had to tread slowly between some prickers or thorny patches that reach out to tear at you? Or have you ever been on a mountain path that forced you to go single file, back to the wall, shuffling your feet sideways so that you could fit?

There are times in your life where taking the smaller gate or narrow path will challenge your pride and even your ability. It will question your resolve and cast doubt on your commitment. It will generate that thing which causes you to want to turn around and go back to the easier way. It will make you something you really don't want to be. It will make you afraid!

Fear is the hedge that keeps us walking the wide path where we're "safe and sound". But God wants us to be more alive then that. He wants us to be excited about life and needs us to be brave enough to love. Will we get hurt? Yes we will. The key thing to remember is that even when we get hurt, we are getting hurt for God, not for ourselves. He promises us that whenever we suffer for him, it is not in vain. He is faithful to heal us and he is very generous with blessing our lives here on Earth and more importantly in our eternal lives to come.

Love is hard work. Nobody can deny that. And love hurts as we venture outside of our comfort zones. But outside our comfort zone is where the real action is. That's where people, young and old alike, pump excitement into their existence and in faith, follow the narrow path that leads back to life the way God planned it. It takes courage to follow God through a small gate and down a narrow road. But take heart in the fact that you are not alone on that road.

Have faith in yourself and trust in God! Be brave enough to set aside comfort for seeking the right path; the one God himself made for you to find and travel on. One of the worlds' most famous poets, Robert Frost, penned one of the worlds' most famous poems about this very dilemma we will all face sometime in our lives; for once we choose a path we may never have the opportunity to change it again, as these last two parts imply;

And both that morning equally lay
In leaves no step had trodden black.
Oh, I kept the first for another day!
Yet knowing how way leads on to way,
I doubted if I should ever come back.

I shall be telling this with a sigh
Somewhere ages and ages hence:
Two roads diverged in a wood, and I--
I took the one less traveled by,
And that has made all the difference

Often the path we choose in younger shoes becomes our life's journey as time seems to slip by without giving pause for changing direction. Our cultural environment and personal experiences lay trail to our order in life and without realizing it; we are older and set in ways we wouldn't necessarily choose given the choice again.

Although there are surely parts of your life right now that would be irresponsible to change, there is still time to change your spiritual direction if you really want to. Leaving behind your wife and children to "find yourself" on a spiritual pilgrimage would be irresponsible. However, leaving behind the comforts of sitting in front of a television with a beer in your hand so that you can do a Bible study with your wife and children is small gate event. Trading a day of golf for a day of volunteer work once in a while is following a narrow path; for many are they on the green and few are those at the soup kitchen!

My point is that although your life may seem mapped out already, you still have a choice. You can choose to find the small gate and travel the narrow path, no matter where you are today. God in his infinite wisdom and grace has provided for us opportunities everywhere we go. Wherever you work, play or live; there somewhere, slightly hidden from the wide path view is a small gate. Look for it. Open it. Leave your comfort zone and begin your walk down the narrow path with God, and as the poet says; - it will make all the difference!

We are only guaranteed now. Yesterday is spent and the future is like clay in our hands. Let's break out of our comfort zones and shape a future that we can brag about when we get to Heaven! Let's learn to love uncomfortably!

Faith Like a Child

"A whole stack of memories never equal one little hope."
Charles M. Schulz

Jesus once said that if we don't come as little children, we will not enter into the Kingdom of Heaven. I don't mean to sound condescending or in any way belittle the point Jesus makes but sometimes I can't help but compare little children to puppies.

To begin with, both little children and puppies seem to be naturally relaxed; that is until something shiny catches their eye and then they are equally quick to get overly excited. The excitement lasts all of two to three seconds at a clip before the infamous glaze comes over their eyes like a rolling fog. You can almost see the question mark pop up over their heads as if to say "what was I doing again?" Then there's the eating and sleeping combo trick. If you're around them long enough you'll catch them actually doing both at the same time. That's what I call entertainment!

Both toddler and pup seem to be totally untroubled by messy, sloppy situations and places; mud is fun and puddles bring pleasure. They also both enjoy a wider range of pliability. Little kids and puppies can easily bend and twist in ways that put some gymnasts to shame. When was the last time you tried touching your toes (let alone chew on your foot) without making a straining noise during the attempt?

If I had to pick a favorite characteristic I'd say the ultimate part of both child and puppy is their innocent spirit of trust. Unlike older members of their species, they don't need to understand something prior to trusting it. One may argue that it's because they haven't yet felt the sting that comes when we get burned by life's many betrayals, and this is certainly true enough. But the fact that we're born with "trusting" souls tells us something regarding our original design. Maybe we were meant to be more trusting.

As children, we are happy to believe in something positive, be it a comic strip hero or holiday gift giver. But as we age, we begin to need to understand what we believe in. No one wants to be a fool. Much like the beloved Charles Shultz Peanuts character Linus, we've all probably had a "Great Pumpkin" experience sometime in our lives, where we truly believed in an unbelievable thing. We may have even defended our beliefs; blindly trusting what we were told was true by those we followed with puppy like faith.

I have to confess that when I was very young I was a

blind faith believer. I absolutely knew that God was always there watching over me. He was watching over everyone I knew; mostly because looking back, everyone I knew also believed. I hadn't met anyone who claimed any different. For a small boy in a Catholic home, going to a Catholic school, believing was a path of no resistance.

An Age of Reasoning

As I got older, I experienced many a proverbial fork in the road. With each one my faith was shaken; sometimes a little bit; sometimes a lot. One of those forks came in the form of a school change in fourth grade. My parents decided to remove us from Catholic school and place us into the public school system. It was there I started meeting other kids my age that were brought up vastly different then I was. They had nicer clothes, newer sneakers and warmer coats then I had. They always had milk money or lunch money and not always in coin form. (Remember, I was born in 1960! It was a different world and a dollar could buy a lot back then!)

These kids seemed very smart and got very good grades. I did notice however that what we covered in second grade in the Catholic school, they were covering in fourth grade in the public school. (Needless to say I sailed through the rest of my Elementary school experience with little effort.)

The kids in Public school seemed to know a lot about a lot of things; but ask some of them about church or God and they returned a blank stare. Some would even break out laughing and say "You really believe all that?" Until that point I never had the slightest doubt that God was real. Even then I still believed; but the concept of other kids not knowing about God and not believing he existed was, well, unbelievable to me.

It was in the sixth grade that I received my first "tenth grade" education. Some of my new found secular friends took great pleasure in sitting me down one day during lunch period where they explained in detail what birds and bees really do. Compared to things today you might consider it a late corruption but it was a corruption all the same. None of us needed to know any of that information but somehow it made its way into our minds. And it seemed that with every bad piece of information entered, a section of innocence in our minds and hearts was deleted.

When it comes to the application of Good and Evil, I believe that we have more power then we think we do. I think that goodness and innocence are of God and they are inherently built into our potential, but Evil is something we're taught. I believe that, much like physical attributes are carried down from generation to generation, so are spiritual attributes. But unlike physical attributes, spiritual attributes in a family can be changed within one generation, even by one person. There is no mistaking the truth that we are unfortunately born into an evil world. There's no escaping the stains of sin we all bear because of the evil around us. We do however have a choice! We can always choose to turn away from evil and pursue a path of goodness and innocence.

For some people the choice for good seems easily brought

out. Some people just seem to be more drawn to goodness and purity. For others, goodness seems to be a struggle. Their personalities lead us to believe that evil would seem to take root much easier. It's as if they were born "bad". An unfortunate truth is that all too often; some parents don't even know or care enough to foster one over the other. Many people raised in dysfunctional environments can't even define good and evil themselves. Much of what they have to go by is what their parents or adult figures have taught them or what they watch on TV which, with every passing year gets farther and farther away from clean examples of good character.

Believing in Innocence

Evil is abundantly evident in our lives. It infiltrates our culture; it degrades our health; it perpetuates our problems and spreads like a virus through our families. Evil brags that it takes but a small stain to ruin the white robe of innocence. Its delight is to leave us feeling hopeless. But evil is wrong! No matter how dark it gets, we only need one small light to follow to guide us out of the darkness.

For those who don't believe in a Creator or a purpose for our lives, that light is a very hard thing to see. But for those who do believe in a loving God, there is always hope. There will always be a light to follow that will lead us out of the darkness and back to goodness and innocence. The key is to believe! As simple and childlike as it sounds, believing is everything. It's that narrow path that we must take to get where we're supposed to go.

In his book entitled "The Marketing of Evil", David Kupelian provides an excellent definition of how our belief fosters a life of faith. He writes:

> "Inside every truly sincere person there is an inner witness, a wordless knowing, a quiet confirmation of all truth. When you reverently inquire into the meaning, not only of the Holy Scriptures, but of everything in life, and - very important – when you have the courage to ***believe*** and hold on to the little glimpses of insight God gives you in response to your sincere searching, you are living by faith."

If we allow the mainstream culture to dictate what we believe, then we are in for trouble. Yet if we earnestly seek the truth, God promises us that the truth will be revealed to us. We may struggle at first as our conscience is re-awakened but if we take the small steps of faith and believe in a real purpose for our lives, we will be led back to a good and innocent path.

I confessed that I started out with a blind faith. The long road I took to get me from that kind of faith to the one I enjoy now was admittedly a painful and confusing one. As a teen I had decided to jump ship from Christianity and into the tidal waters of popular spirituality. I read books by Edgar Cayce and Lobsang Rampa and many others who delved deeply into the metaphysical mysticism of the spirit world. I sat with Spiritual Channels and was told about previous lives I've lived, and how those lives led me to the life I was currently living.

As hard as I tried to find God and the truth in all of it, I couldn't get any further then the belief that there was indeed such a thing as the spirit world. That didn't come as much comfort. The fact is that, as I moved my search forward, I more often felt fear instead of peace and my experiences left me with more questions then answers.

I investigated all the main world religions. I wanted to know where they originated and why other people believed them. I could find parts of each that made sense but they all eventually unraveled into a pile of contradictions and unanswerable questions that demanded me to go back to the starting point of blind faith to accept them. That was a place I refused to go.

I contemplated the arguments of atheism for a short time. But the thought of all this; the world we live in, from sub atomic science to the solar system our planet resides in, to the universe that our solar system is dwarfed by, is all so amazingly designed that it seemed to take much more faith than I could ever muster to believe it was all actually random and pointless.

Eventually I came full circle and began to study Christianity again. After searching everywhere else, I figured I had nothing to lose; only this time I looked at every possible argument my thoughts could find. For the first time in my life I read the entire Holy Bible; and not just a "Good News" version but a solid study version with maps, concordance, dictionary, practical application notes, biographies and a comprehensive index section.

I read books on Christian Apologetics by people who had the very same questions and doubts about Christianity I did and set out to disprove its truth; only to find that there was real evidence for most everything claimed in the pages of those sixty six books, written over thousands of years by a multitude of authors; all claiming to be inspired by the same God.

I was amazed to find the extensive archeological work done in the Middle East that unlayered location after location recorded in those books. Although some places in the Bible are still unverified and labeled as "possible sites", most of the locations are places you can find on a map and go visit today. In a post modern world, the thought that all paths lead to God is illogical and irrational. The more I studied, the more I was convinced that the Bible was an accurate historical record and that Jesus was the Messiah that the books of old prophesied about. The evidence is overwhelmingly in support of the truth of the Gospels.

So my faith took a leap; only this time it wasn't blind. This time my faith was based on a lot of provable facts and common sense conclusions. I no longer had to guess or take the word of others for what I was to believe. I had sound and solid information to base my faith upon. But now came the hard part. Now before me was a journey that many a scholar will set out to take; only to allow their pride laden intellect lead them to failure. It is a vast span; a life distance;

one that can't even be measured in miles. But it can be measured in inches!

With all the knowledge I gained and data I gathered and statistics I reviewed, I knew in my mind that Christianity was a sound religion and worthy of believing. Yet Christianity, at its core is not about a religion; it's about a relationship isn't it? I needed to take what I knew in my mind and move it down about eighteen inches and secure it in my heart; because faith isn't a mind thing, it's a heart thing; a heart thing that turns us back towards innocence. And innocence brings us back to the child within and realigns us to our original design.

Children of God

Innocence is a wonderful thing. The word itself has multiple meanings to us. The Merriam-Webster dictionary defines innocence as;

- Freedom from guilt or sin through being unacquainted with evil
- Blamelessness
- freedom from legal guilt of a particular crime or offense
- freedom from guile or cunning
- lack of worldly experience or sophistication
- lack of knowledge

Going back to the child-puppy analogy I made at the beginning of the chapter, is it easy to understand, judging by these definitions, why the common belief is that children are innocent. Much like Adam and Eve before the apple tree experience, children simply don't "know" evil. They are still free from the experience of it. They are, as the first definition puts it; unacquainted with evil. What would you give to have that kind of freedom? Imagine how much less stress you would have in your life if you could forget about all the evil in the world.

I realize what I am asking sounds like I'm promoting ignorance. And in a literal way you could say that's true as the base word here is "ignore". I'm not saying we should forget evil and act like it isn't there. Much like fire, if we are blind to it but get too close to it, we will get burned! What I am saying is that we can try to ignore its lure and fight our fascination with it. Like the con man at a carnival, we can choose to turn away from it so that we don't risk loss.

The key to being successful at this is to establish exactly what evil is and is not. There can be no gray area like the one today's culture promotes. That's why it is crucial for us to turn to God's word for direction. Our Heavenly Father loves us more then we can imagine and has given us basic, common sense instructions to live by so that we can not only survive, but thrive in the world.

As a father, one of the most repeated phrases I've used over the years is this: "Just do what you're told!" I'd tell my boys time and again that if they just did what they were told, they would stay out of trouble. It sounds easy, doesn't it? Don't lie, don't cheat, don't steal, don't hurt each other, remember your manners and treat others as you want to be treated. "And when I tell you to do something, just do it." Simple enough, right? But here's where they would lose it every time....they would say, "But I thought if I did this..." or "I don't see why I had to do that..." Can you see where it broke down? The fundamental problem was a lack of trust in their father. They would think to themselves about what they wanted verses what I wanted and would decide that they trusted their decisions over my direction.

They never rebelled that way when they were younger. When they were "Little Children" they would do whatever I told them to do. Life was simplistic then. As hectic as it was sometimes, things always seemed to be in control and we had a lot of fun. Would they misbehave at times? Of course they would. And like a loving parent I would discipline them when needed, always reminding them that I love them even when they're in trouble.

Like my kids as they got older, the real trouble starts for us when we decide that we know better then our Father and we stop doing what we're told, thinking we have the right to be disobedient. We wrestle control out of his hands and we run around like kids with sharp objects, just begging for trouble. We think we know what we're doing but we really don't, and that's a huge problem!

Like Jesus implied as he prayed from the cross for his father to forgive us; know matter what we think we know, we don't know that we don't know what we're doing. We are blind to the dangers and evil of this world and we only make things worse when we allow our foolish pride to dictate our disciplines.

We all need to be like the little children. This doesn't mean we need to be blindly following God, like inexperienced puppies; full of trust and lacking in sense. We just need to do what we're told by God, our loving and caring father who really knows what's best for us in life.

There is more than enough information out there for anyone truly seeking, to find the truth and be educated in it. There's absolutely no excuse to check your brains at the door of the church. We need critical thinkers in the body of Christ. That said, we need all the more to be a body that does what the head says.

There are things we may not understand or even agree with. That doesn't mean they are wrong. And if God, the Creator of this awesome universe we live in, is willing to guide us with his Word and Spirit, then we should, for God's sake as well as our own, practice faith like little children and do what we are told. If we do, we will have much less stress and much more security. When we do, we open ourselves to the opportunity to re-learn innocence, as we seek His guidance and learn to love the way He loves.

Sick and Tired of Being Sick and Tired

"...I need You, need your help. I can't do this myself; you're the only one who can undo what I've become."
Rush of Fools

I still remember the huge Willow tree we used to have in our yard growing up. Its sweeping branches were strong enough for a lightweight like me to swing on. I would grab a handful and, starting at one end and then I would run a stretch of the perimeter and then jump! It was amazing! I would swing about thirty feet before I had to just kick my feet to the ground, enabling an additional twenty five feet of free flight. We eventually tied a tire swing to one of the bigger branches which allowed us to swing "inside" the tree as well. I could do that for hours it seemed. I would run as hard as I could and then at the last second, jump high and grab a knot that was strategically placed for maximum lift. My butt would land on the tire and I'd lean way back and just soak in the blurry kaleidoscope of images swirling passed my eyes as I relaxed and enjoyed the ride.

If I wasn't swinging on the Willow tree I was climbing one of the Maples. They are a fun tree to climb; a bit more challenging then the Pines we had and harder to hide in. If you want to hide, don't pick a Maple. But my all time favorites were the Pine trees that we had in the front yard. They grew to about seventy feet tall and their branches were like rungs on a ladder. As soon as I was tall enough to jump and grab the lowest branch, I climbed them all the way to the top. I loved it up there. I could see the top of my house and all the houses around us. I could see my brothers and sisters below, like ants crawling on the ground. Sometimes I would hear them calling me and I'd call back but they never knew where I was.

What Happened to Us?

Life seemed so simple back then. There was time for work and time for play; time to eat and time to sleep. There was right and wrong and depending on the side we chose, there was reward or there was punishment. Back then my mind seemed to possess a clarity that I find harder to enjoy now that I'm older and supposedly wiser. What used to be black and white has now been somehow sifted, screened and categorized into folders of every shade of gray imaginable.

Where did the clarity go? Why is it so hard nowadays for us to see the defining line between good and bad or right and wrong? And what is this incessant weight that seems ever present on our hearts and minds, causing perpetual stress in our lives?

There seems to be an epidemic of stress and worry spreading across America. And it's not just limited to grown ups with jobs and bills. It appears to be affecting almost every age group we have, save our youngest. Anxiety Disorders Association of America posted the following statistics on their website:

> Anxiety disorders are the most common mental illness in the U.S., affecting 40 million adults in the United States age 18 and older (18.1% of U.S. population).
>
> Anxiety disorders cost the U.S. more than $42 billion a year, almost one-third of the country's $148 billion total mental health bill, according to "The Economic Burden of Anxiety Disorders," a study commissioned by ADAA and published in The Journal of Clinical Psychiatry, Vol. 60, No. 7, July 1999

The statistic of 18% of the adult U.S. population being affected by anxiety is absolutely staggering! What happened to us? How did we get so sick? And more importantly, how do we get ourselves better?

What is creating all the stress in our lives? While the experts list a variety of causes and offer solid solutions to deal with a lot of them, there will always be the one cause that only God's love and direction can cure. I speak of that deep insecurity that grows inside us as we are tossed around in the storm of relativism. We were created to exist in a world where most issues are black and white. The problem is that in the culture of relativism we live in, we are forced to see everything in grays which cause confusion and depression.

Indecision is a troublesome thing when we're looking for a new car or picking a restaurant to go to on a Friday night. It can cause wasted time, lost opportunity and frustration. But compared to things of the spirit and morality, these daily grays are nothing. We work hard and pay taxes and try our best to plan for the future. We invest ourselves into our children and grandchildren in hopes that their future will be better then our past. But what will the future look like and who are the players shaping it? More importantly, what is the foundation that our future rests on?

Our nation was founded on very solid Judeo-Christian principles. Since it's inception we have struggled to maintain those principles while striving to grow economically and culturally. We've made huge mistakes in the past when we've forsaken our responsibilities as stewards of the land and protectors of all peoples. Our twentieth century was a leap from hard work and simple life to hard work and complex life. Technology has both blessed and cursed us as we struggle to use it to understand the many illnesses we caused while advancing it. Too often we've cut corners and destroyed nature for the sake of advancement rather then learning from nature to find solutions.

I don't bring all this up just to bash America for her mistakes. I love this country and I'm very proud of its position in the world as a strong leader and the most generous country in history. We've done more for hunger and sickness then any other nation or civilization and we need to always be mindful of that. But it's exactly that fact that supports my belief that we are a great nation precisely because we are a good people. And agree or not, we are a good people because we were founded on strong Judeo-Christian values.

Throughout the first two centuries of our young history we've been blessed to have many Christian and other God respecting immigrants come to our land, deepening the collective faith in our culture. However, as generations pass and we drift away from these values, we begin to marginalize our greatness and bring to question the validity of our goodness.

Then and Now

Most of the original Ivy League schools were built to teach the Holy Bible with the intent of educating and evangelizing America. The founders knew that a nation that is reverent to God will be a civilized and prosperous nation. All throughout the first century the Holy Bible was the standard textbook used to teach reading, spelling, composition skills, world history and basic rules of proper living.

By-in-large communities thrived with low crime and high degrees of charity.

Compare this with today where our schools aren't allowed to speak of God but are allowed to hand out condoms. Children aren't allowed to read books about Jesus and his teachings but they are forced in some cases to read "Tommy has two Mommies". Our colleges intentionally avoid the hope and purpose found in studying Intelligent Design. Instead they preach as fact the patchy theory of Evolution and the pointlessness of life, other than just surviving. All this education is topped with a sugary glaze of "there's really no absolute right or wrong…most things are relative!" It's no wonder we're sick!

The bible gives us two important things; examples to learn from and guidance to follow. Throughout the entire Old Testament we see example after example of how God blesses cultures that heed his guidance while destruction falls on those who ignore it. We can argue forever on the vast cultural differences that are evident when comparing then and now. We can also go through years of line item topics where the people of that day could have or should have, but refused to stop doing things we would all agree is wrong in today's world.

However, even with those differences, there are still many core similarities that we can and should learn from. The overriding truth of it all is that when people and nations follow the God of Abraham, they prosper. When they don't, they end up depraved or manipulated by toxic tyranny which spills over, causing damage to others.

At this point some might say "Well what about the Jews? Haven't they suffered through most of their existence even though they are supposedly God's chosen people?" The answer is yes they have; every time they've strayed from God's plan and direction. But he's forever faithful to lead them back and heal them when they repent. Others may ask "What about the Muslims? Doesn't the Koran point to the same Allah God of Abraham, Isaac and Jacob; yet one might argue that the Islamic religion is one of violence and intolerance?" The answer again is yes it does point to the very same God but it unfortunately goes on to also distort the true love of God by asking followers to kill unbelievers. That's not God's plan.

Still many would throw up a red flag here and say that at our core we're still a Christian nation with one of the best governments in all of history, and yet we still suffer many social problems. To that I would ask this question. On average, do our elected officials really put others first and themselves last as Jesus teaches? Do they make sure the widow and the orphan are taken care of before enjoying their mansions and their boundless benefits and perks? Are the laws that Congress pass always aligned with what God says or do they more often cater to Lobbyists? Apart from the grass roots community and various Church support systems, can anyone really say our "government" is currently based on the teachings of Jesus and the love and grace of God?

My point in all this is that if we study history we clearly see a pattern of blessing when people really pay attention to God's word and really live by it, versus the curse of destruction when people stray from God and place themselves in charge instead. Whenever man has worshipped other gods or set himself up as a god demanding mass allegiance, the system inevitably caves in on itself. Even today the only real pockets of hope across the globe are found in groups actively working according to Jesus' teachings even if some of them don't claim his name.

If we are to ever truly heal this land; if we are to thrive as a people and be a nation set apart, we must return to the fundamental teachings found in the Bible. I understand the argument against "forcing" one religion on the masses and I agree whole heartedly that this argument is a valid one. If Jesus refused to force his will on others then who are we to do it? But we don't need to throw the baby out with the bath water. Jesus was the most influential man who ever lived and for very good reason. He taught us how to love! We all need to know how to love the right way; not just anyone's way and surely not the way the world teaches. There is some truth in the question some would ask; "Who am I to force my morality on them?" The answer is I'm nobody at all.

The fact is that there is only one perfect man whose teachings lead to peace and hope. Of all the definitions people conjure up to define love, there is only one perfect example. It's not mine and it's not yours. It's His. It's Gods!

He created it. He sustains it. Most importantly, He shares it with us and teaches us the truth and the way to share it with others.

I, for one, am sick and tired of being sick and tired. I want to enjoy life the way it was originally designed to be. I may never be able to experience the fullness of life as God planned it here on this Earth now, but I have every confidence that God will come at the end of days to heal Creation and heal us too.

I believe we will see a new Heaven and a new Earth and we will all know and practice the very perfect love of God. On that day; that eternally endless day you and I may meet and effortlessly share the greatest of love with the Creator of life. I hope for that.

Until that day we are all left with a choice. We can look to each other for answers or we can look to God. My prayer is that Americans realize, before it's too late, that love is something we need to get absolutely right and that we once again accept God's guidance to that endeavor. I pray that before our nation falls too far, we turn and repent, humbly admit our faults and ask for God's grace to once again bring us to the righteous path again.

And finally, I pray with my all my heart that we once again take pride in the words "God Bless America". More then that I pray that the eternal record shows us as one nation whose final summation and purpose was that America Blessed God!

Divided We Fall

"Every kingdom divided against itself will be ruined, and every city or household divided against itself will not stand."
Jesus of Nazareth

There are few things more impressive to watch in school sports then Crew (otherwise known as Rowing). As spectators we are privileged to see a tightly knit team of up to nine people working together like a fine oiled machine, moving with one mind across a placid water span. From an aerial view the boat looks like a water bug skimming the top of the water in a symphony of interconnected, simultaneous motions. The success of the team is in direct proportion to the synchronicity of their movements.

At the helm (or more technically, the stern) is the Stroke. The Stroke is the person responsible for setting the pace and rhythm of the team. It is this persons' job to throttle the collective power of the rowers to maximize speed, without corrupting the smooth feeling of the boat's travel. The group of people participating in this sport can be as diverse as a New York City street crowd on any given day; but when they are in that boat, they are one. They aren't thinking about their individual life problems or dreaming about individual life pursuits. They are focused and submissive to the team activity at hand. Crew is truly a symbolic testament to what we as a species can accomplish if we all get on the same page with a unified direction.

I think it's important to point out that even as evident as it is that this is a Team sport, it's still made up of individuals who choose to follow a leader and an individual that chooses to lead a following of teammates. As tight as the teamwork must be, it still boils down to individual decisions on the part of every person on the team to put show-boating aside (no pun intended) and work together to bring everyone a win.

I think that our spirituality was supposed to be a lot more like Crew then we've allowed it to be. I believe that God intended us to work together in harmony rather then have an endless list of different religions and fractioned sects. He did create us as individuals and does want us all to have an individual relationship with him. But it seems to me that the original intent was for us to work together as a team to bring humanity to a win. Unfortunately we are a stubborn people who allow pride and envy to corrupt the smooth flow of our love.

In most races, there is really one correct direction to go to win, or at the very minimum, finish the race. Could you imagine the chaotic comedy of a city marathon if, when the starting gun was fired, everyone took off in whatever direction they felt like? Barring serious injuries and any race induced traffic jams, the scene would be very funny to watch from the safety of a 3rd floor window. One thing we could count on in this scenario is that just a small fraction of the racers would find the finish line.

If we stop to think about it, wouldn't it seem as though the collective spiritual experience of mankind is really playing out like that? If our eternal lives really depend on finishing this race then I vote against the hap-hazard method of letting us all "find our own way".

What if we were all put into this world by a loving God who tries his best to show us the right direction, knowing there's only one that really counts. Would it be his fault when we lose because we refuse to listen and we prefer defining our own race track instead?

Taking Direction

What if this world is designed to be a spiritual launch pad and our souls are like rockets that shoot off into eternity once they achieve the required amount of catalyst. Of all the directions allowed in the vastness of space, what if there is but one correct path that leads to our true destination. What if we have only one chance to point the rocket in the right direction before liftoff? If we make a mistake in our calculations we're sunk because there's no way to change coarse once we've blasted off.

Here's an idea for a model. Take a golf ball and drill a small hole in it. Get a straight piece of wire and stick it in the hole. Try to imagine the ball is our world and the wire is your launch trajectory. Now examine that ball. I mean really look hard at it. How many possible directions can you go coming off that little world you hold in your hand? If you draw one straight line around the circumference you would theoretically end up with 360 options, barring fractional degrees. 360!!! If we used ½ degrees it would be 720 options of which way you could go. That's scary! But not as scary as the other tens of thousands of options you have to pick from to get it right.

The craziest thing about all this is that God himself spells out the exact point that we're supposed to launch from; the exact direction we are to take. Yet for many of us here on this beautiful blue ball, we choose to ignore Gods' direction and guidance, and instead follow our own ideas of which way we should go. So many people fall for the age old lie that we don't need God; that we ourselves are like gods and we can use our own wisdom to find the enlightened path. More than ever, right now is a great time to ask ourselves how that plan is working out for us.

I'm sure many of you are thinking about the arrogance of Christianity in claiming to be "the only way" to get back to God. There are many different holy books in print that clearly offer other paths to follow without having to submit to a life of subservience. We ask the same questions over and over. Isn't it true that all paths ultimately lead to the same place? Aren't all gods but an expression of One; the very oneness that all life flows from and returns to? Can't we seek out and find our true selves from within? Does it really matter which path we take or where we get answers from as long as we try our best to be good people? The answer is YES IT MATTERS!

God never intended for us to make up our own rules or religions. He never said to look within for the answers. He knows just how perverse and corrupt our "within" is. Instead he gave us sound commandments to follow; the very first of which is to put him first in our lives. The truth is that if we just get that part right, then everything else will fall into place. But knowing our selfish human nature, God laid out a very specific path for us to follow to get back to him. That path is called Immanuel. The word literally means "God with us." God loves us so much that, unlike any other god or king in history, he gave up his throne to come live with us and physically show us the way.

He proved his love and his awesome control of life itself when he willingly died on a cross for all peoples and then resurrected himself three days later. He even stayed with us (humanity) for forty more days so that there was ample opportunity for us to see, believe and document this pivotal point in human history.

If you were to turn on your TV today and see reporters interviewing hundreds of people who all told the same version of a story, wouldn't you think it was true? If that story jived with the local governments' accounting of many of the facts they themselves were a part of, would you give credence to the story as being factual? Yet this is exactly what happened when Jesus came into the world to bare the punishment for our sins.

He came, he taught many, he healed many, he resurrected the dead in front of many, he spoke with authority to the religious leaders of the day and then he willingly died at their hands. After three days the evidence puts forth that over 500 people saw him alive as he encouraged them to believe in a loving God and accept his sacrifice as their atonement.

Shortly after leaving our world, God sent us a helper, just as he promised he would. On the day of Pentecost the Holy Spirit fell upon the disciples and transformed them from panic stricken hideouts to bold public witnesses. They picked right up where Jesus left off. They healed many, they resurrected the dead in front of many; and they spread the Gospel or Good News of Gods' love and redeeming power through faith in Jesus, the long awaited Messiah. From that day to this, those who actually follow Christ's teachings and live to serve God and others, more then themselves, bare witness to the fact that Jesus is still very much alive and well.

Doubters would ask, "If Jesus is still alive then why can't we see him?" To that I would answer that if everything is made up of sub atomic particles then why can't we see them? If the wind can take down a tree then why can't we see the wind?

If our thoughts and feelings are real then why can't we see them? There is an endless supply of examples to pick from. Many life changing and life sustaining entities are unseen yet we would all bet our farms on their reality. My point is that maybe we need to stop thinking so small.

Maybe if we step out of the batting box of this physical world and move towards the first base of the meta-physical, then we would have a chance to really make it home again. God is our coach. He defined the diamond and laid out the bases. He is there signaling us to run; not away from him but towards him. Many will drop the bat and run the other way, rather then do what he asks. For that metaphorical fact our humanity will lose this game; even if a small fraction of players do make it home.

It's not Gods' fault that so many turn from him. It isn't his fault that we are so divided in our beliefs. If you've ever read the bible or have a working knowledge of the basics of it, you'd have to agree that God has done all he can do to lead us to himself, yet the decision will always be ours to make. There are times when I feel very sad for what our human race put the Creator through. My heart breaks for God; that he has done so much, yet on the average, we care so little. But then I remember how very little we are.

Seeing our Smallness

The first chapter of Hebrews shares a thought provoking truth for us to ponder. It says in verses one and two;

> "In the past God spoke to our forefathers through the prophets at many times and in various ways, but in these last days he has spoken to us by his Son, whom he appointed heir of all things, and through whom he made the universe."

When astronomers talk about our universe they use an adjective to more accurately portray it. They place the word "known" before the word universe because they are fully aware that our technical capabilities are still somewhat limited. In the mind of pretty much everyone; there is no doubt, more out there then we currently have the ability to see.

Just so we have some basics down, we measure space in a metric called "light years". A light year is the distance light will travel in a 365 day year. Light, as you may know, travels at a speed of 186 thousand miles per second or roughly 671 million miles per hour. So let's do some math;

> 365(days) x 24(hrs per day) x 671 million (mph) =
> 5 trillion, 788 billion, 960 million miles per light year

Wasn't that fun? Now with that figure in mind, consider this estimated fact; the edge of the "known" universe is approximately…are you ready?...46.5 BILLION LIGHT YEARS AWAY!! I'm not even going to attempt the math on 46,500,000,000 times 5,788,960,000,000. If I did, my head would blow clean off my shoulders! It wouldn't be pretty!

Somewhere in the middle of this unbelievable expanse

we call our known universe, there is a tiny thing called the Milky Way Galaxy. This tiny spec in the known universe is a mere 100,000 light years in diameter and only about 1000 light years thick. Not much compared to the "grand" scheme of things. But let's not stop there. Let's look at where we are in this proverbial spec. Our Earth is estimated to be about 26,000 light years from the center of the Milky Way galaxy. The Solar System in which our planet spins is roughly 7.35 billion miles across. It's not very big really; a mere .001 light years across.

I will say this; anyone doubting the theory of intelligent design should do a quick study of all the factors that play into our exact location in the galaxy. You will walk away from the data in awe! So many things have to line up in such a tight order for life to exist that it's statistically impossible for life to exist; unless someone designed it to.

Hebrews continues to hint at the actual size of God in chapter 4, verse 13 where Paul says:

> "Nothing in all creation is hidden from God's sight. Everything is uncovered and laid bare before the eyes of him to whom we must give account."

Try if you can to imagine a God so big that the whole universe (not just the part we know about) is laid out before him like a piece of paper for him to read. Every part of it at every level is plainly revealed to him who formed it all in the palm of his hands.

Louie Giglio created a "Passion Talk Series" that includes

an incredible, awe inspiring DVD presentation he titles "Indescribable". In it he demonstrates, far better then I can do here, the infinitely boundless size of God. Here's what he says to a crowd in Houston, Texas as he shares his thoughts. He says:

> "I'm not saying all this to make you feel small. I'm saying all this to remind you that you ARE small!"

This guy is good! With that one phrase he hit the nail right on the head. Who do we really think we are anyway? We are so small compared to the size of our planet. Our planet is like a tiny piece of dust floating in a stadium sized galaxy. Our galaxy is but one of hundreds of billions in the known universe....all of which is held in the palm of a loving creator God.

Is it no wonder why we would fall when we separate ourselves from God? When we choose to deny him and ignore his love for us, we become like a spec of dry skin floating on his arm. We have no life, no hope, and most of all, no real purpose. Why wouldn't he just brush us off? What does he, the creator of all things, owe any of us? And as if it's not obvious by now, hasn't he already given us far more then we could ever deserve?

All this said; never forget that as infinitely small as we are, God still knows each of us by name. We'll never be able to grasp the vastness of his love but we can certainly have faith in it. We can also strive to have faith in each other, and in that, share the vastness of his love with one another. It may sound weird or even hard, but it isn't really. Stop judging. Stop preconditioning. Stop looking through your eyes and try to see through the lens of God. He sees us as one human race; no division. We need to start seeing ourselves the same way and caring in a way that reflects the wholeness of humanity.

We can do this. We need him and we need each other, but we can really do this. We were designed to; to love each other. We are so small yet he cares about us and he gives us the capacity to care about each other in the same way. If we can ratchet back the pride, turn up the humility a bit and then just follow his lead, we can find a way to love each other, and in the process, find our way home. I don't know about you but to a puny punk like me, that sounds like an excellent deal!

A New Year

"How few there are who have courage enough to own their faults, or resolution enough to mend them."
Benjamin Franklin

As I write this chapter, our world is celebrating the end of 2009 and the beginning of 2010. It appears we survived the first decade of the new millennium. As I sat watching the many cities across the globe ring in the New Year, I couldn't help but think of the staggering amounts of money our world spends on all the celebratory activities each year. Between all the planning, travel, security, entertainment, food and drink and clean up, we must collectively spend billions on this one night.

One of the most amazing things about New Years Eve is that the whole planet seems to be focused on the same thing, even if for just this one day a year. As the earth turns and clocks strike midnight, we take our turns like a slow moving group wave in a stadium, raising our hands and hearts to the memories of the past and all the new beginnings another year will bring. No matter what your belief system, political point of view, age or intellect, you can believe in, and confess to the start of a new year for the world. Admittedly, there those who follow a different calendar but in a world economy, everything is tied together, one way or the other. Rarely is there anything else that happens for the next 364 days that grabs such universal attention.

So I got to thinking last night as I watched the massive global celebration; I wonder how all the extremely poor people in places like Africa are celebrating? I wonder ***if*** they are celebrating. I mean why wouldn't they be? Aren't they part of our human race? Even in their daily struggles, they must appreciate the fact that they survived another year, and for some, another decade!

I wonder what God is thinking on New Year's Eve as he looks down and see's his people spending exorbitant amounts of "blessing" on a virtual one night stand while his others, in such desperate need, struggle to survive. I also wonder if we (the Church) will ever get organized enough to take all that blessing (money) that we spend on New Years Eve and for just one year, give it to all the organizations that struggle to help the poor every day. Imagine if World Vision, Compassion International, Habitat for Humanity or any of the other not for profit Aid groups got a one billion dollar check on January first?

Before I go on I think it only right to say that there are many people and congregations that do an outstanding job reaching out to the poor, both domestically and abroad. To all of you I say "well done, good and faithful servants." I also need to admit that I am every bit as guilty here as the next Christian. I eat, I drink, I play and dance and wait up until the ball drops. Then I make a bunch of post midnight calls to loved ones, wishing them a Happy New Year. I have to confess that I didn't pause to remember all my brothers and sisters in Christ, living eight thousand miles away, who do without all the basic things I take for granted. But I should have!

If I want water I go to the faucet. If I'm hungry, I go to the refrigerator. If I'm cold, I turn up the heat or go to the closet where I have at least fifty options of clothes to wear. And if I'm a bit too warm, then I always have my Central Air. If my tooth hurts, I call a dentist. If I feel sick, I call a doctor. If I'm seriously wounded, I can even have a trained medical team come to my house with a tricked out medical van, in which they will personally escort me to the nearest hospital. All just a wireless phone call away! God Bless America!

Compare these "basics" to the basics of our Christian brothers and sisters on the other side of the planet. And make no mistake, in the eyes of God; they are every bit our brothers and sisters as our blood relatives are. If they want water, they grab a container and walk from mere yards to miles to get it, and when they do, it is most likely contaminated with parasites. If they are hungry, they deal with the pain, sometimes for days.

Most people have only one or two garments to wear. There is no climate control so they will have to suffer both heat and cold. There is no accessible medical help or preventative medication without walking for hours or days, if it's available at all. Even our most insignificant and preventable injuries and sicknesses are daily death threats to these poor people. There are no eye drops for Pink Eye or ear drops for ear infections. These low level illnesses lead to blindness and loss of hearing. A simple cut on their bare feet could end up maiming them due to the high risk of infection.

Where our children learn to read and write by first grade, their children learn to labor in the sun and act as fill-in parental figures for their siblings as their parents are ravaged by horrible diseases like Malaria, Tuberculosis and HIV/AIDS. AIDS in poor countries is very different from AIDS in America. There are many who look at AIDS as a "Gay" disease. The reality is that AIDS is, for the most part, a heterosexually transmitted disease. I believe that the church as a whole needs to stop viewing this as a "punishment for promiscuity" and start viewing it as a call to arms to help the orphan and the widow.

Please don't get me wrong. I'm not saying that God "gave us" AIDS to test our obedience, let alone punish anyone. But I am very sure that He is calling on us to help reduce and destroy it. He is calling on the "blessed" of the world to help those in need. With today's technology, it is very easy to find where the greatest need is. It took me about five minutes to pull up some comparison statistics for some countries in Africa versus where we in the U.S.A. stand. The stats are sobering!

Country	Population	<$1/day	ALE*	IMR**
Burkina Faso	13.9 million	45%	48.5	9.2%
Ethiopia	74.7 million	23%	49	9.4%
Ghana	22.4 million	23%	59.5	5.5%
Kenya	34.7 million	23%	49	5.9%
Rwanda	8.6 million	52%	47	9.0%
Tanzania	37.4 million	49%	45.5	9.6%
Uganda	28.2 million	85%	60	6.6%
USA	304 million	0%	78	0.63%

<$1/day = Living on less then a dollar a day
* = Average Life Span
** = Infant Mortality Rate
Data taken from Compassion International and Wikipedia Websites

Obviously, there is a huge disparity between our richness and their poverty. When looking at this data, we need to start with the simple fact of geography. The worlds' poor would be as rich as we are if they happened to be born in the USA. And the scary truth is that we would be as poor as they, had we been born in their location. Do we really want to blame them for their poverty? There are those who would argue that God is in control and since he put them their, it isn't our responsibility. I do agree that God is in control. In fact we need to remember that everything we have; our health, money, and prosperity are His, not ours. He entrusts us with His blessings and commands us to share them. The measure of our sharing isn't supposed to be what we think we can afford, rather it should be whatever it takes to take care of our brothers and sisters of humanity.

Again, I am proud of how some in America have answered the call to help. There are many good and caring people, both Christian and Non-Christian who sacrifice daily to support the needs of those in less fortunate positions, both here and abroad. But I can't help but look at the big picture and feel we're still missing something.

The Measure of Wealth

It's a very interesting time to be in America. We seem to be at the start of an initiative to change our fundamental way of governing from a Capitalistic to a Socialistic platform. I'm sure we could argue all day for either side, so for now, I'll just stay out of it. To me, the platform we choose is not nearly as important as the motives behind the agendas. At our core, we the people, tend to be selfish. In my humble opinion, ***that*** is the crux of our problem.

The Bible can be interpreted to support either platform, although both modern day platforms seem to misplace the biblical message and instruction. The long history of world governments reflects that equality and the good of humanity come secondary to the possession of power and control of wealth. When everyone has their basic needs met before anyone has excess, then I think we're collectively starting from the right place. It's convincing the world to see and act that way that is the problem. Unless all nations learn to love the way Jesus taught, we will continue to delay real success for humanity in our world.

There has been a lot of discussion in America in 2009

about "redistribution" of wealth. Wealth is defined by most as W = A – L, or Wealth = Assets – liabilities. So the logical question would be; what are our assets and what are our liabilities. The answers are relatively easy to arrive at when you're only talking about money. But as members of the human race, is that all we choose to see?

What is the value of a happy and healthy child? What is the value of a parent; better yet both parents who are educated and responsible? What are the assets and liabilities in promoting health in a third world village? Isn't a vaccine much cheaper then treatment? And of those vaccinated who can now learn or work because they're healthy; would they not add to the value of a society?

These are common sense questions that I feel guilty even asking because to ask would imply people don't know. Of course we all know what the better scenario is. It doesn't matter what part of the world you live in, the answers to these questions are evident. Helping the poorest of our world would be to the benefit of all people. What we lack, here in this country, as well as other nations and even within the church, is the will to come together and commit to whatever it takes to fix the problems.

A common response to discussions like this is that the problems are so big and wide spread; how can one person, one church or even one country make a difference? The answer is in the reason for writing this book! We all need to love like God loves! I'm not foolish enough to suggest we need to convert the entire world to one religion. What I'm saying is even if you are an atheist or any other faith, Jesus is still the very best example of how everyone on the planet should practice love. The more people that make the decision to love as God loves, the more power we will have in driving real change. Every one of us has the ability to help in some way and at a grass roots level, many of us do. Unfortunately at the leadership level, it is a tragically different story.

I may be wrong about my interpretation of the priorities that our governments, lawyers and corporate leaders hold, but it seems to me that, on the average, accumulating individual wealth is far more important then using it for the good of mankind. For that matter, it seems that their God given skills and abilities are also somewhat misguided. Many act as though everyone is born equally blessed with a fair shake in life and that somehow they've risen above others all by themselves. It wasn't God who made them smart or blessed their steps in life; they did it. They are responsible for every good attribute they possess. They somehow feel entitled to all that they have, and believe they "deserve" a better life then everyone else. It's the age old error made by many people born with advantage. They think the advantage they were blessed with is there to be used for selfish reasons.

But for the grace of God, we would all be born in Burkina Faso or Rwanda. We would all be malnourished, dehydrated and parasite ridden. We would all be victims of horrible plagues with unspeakable suffering. I'm not trying to remove credit from people who do make the most of the blessings; mental, physical and material, that they have been given. If you have the wonderful honor of a great education and are in good health, then I am truly happy for you. But you need to always remember that these are blessings from God, entrusted to you to help mankind with. In God's eyes, they aren't "yours", but His. He is allowing you the honor of enjoying them while giving you the responsibility to use them for good.

It's OK to have a beautiful house, nice car and whatever else you really like. But don't store up wealth that would carry you for generations. Give the extra to those in need, and God will give you eternal riches that will bless your family for generations to come. You can still be rich. God likes that. But don't hoard it; spread it around. Take pleasure in blessing others as God has blessed you; in doing so you honor God's trust in your stewardship and you store up treasures in Heaven.

I don't begrudge anyone from prosperity. I just think we need to re-evaluate how and why some are compensated for their services. When you compare the compensation given to your Senator or Congressman against that of a Head Nurse at your local hospital, and then think about their individual contributions to you and your community; you can't help but wonder if things are, as Fox News says, "fair and balanced!" Especially since the Head Nurse can't arbitrarily vote herself a salary increase.

Serving your country as a people's representative is an

honor and privilege, and should require the highest degree of humility and moral character. Jesus' greatest attribute as a leader was that, in his heart of hearts, he was a humble servant. He had the chance to amass wealth and political power but instead, he used his talents to bring hope and teach the true meaning of love. He may have died without real estate or a bank account, but he certainly wasn't poor in his Father's eyes.

Jesus didn't claim political power; instead he claimed the power of love and forgiveness, which has grown as a Christian movement for the last two thousand years; across every continent on the planet. Historically speaking, he is the most influential man who ever lived, and that has nothing to do with material wealth. If that's not power, I don't know what is. Yet he never abused his power over the people, as do many a politician and national leader of this age.

Unlike the Corporate, Finance and Judicial systems in America, and all the lawyers who get rich off them, Jesus always stood for what was right and true and not just profitable. He promoted unselfish support of people with compassion and justice based on God's will. He wasn't swayed by money or position, yet he could be easily moved at the sight of a poor widow or orphan.

Unlike divorce lawyers who see dollar signs in family breakdowns, Jesus saw the true value of people and the asset they can be to each other in love, if they would put the needs of others before the wants of themselves. I should say, in their defense, that if people put God first and loved their spouses as they love themselves, we wouldn't need divorce lawyers. It's not really their fault that there's such a high demand for their services. That said, many really over capitalize on the unfortunate opportunity and for that, they add to the overall problem.

Allow me to put it in a less confrontational, symbolic manner. Try to imagine yourself as a cup sitting in a flower bed. God's blessings and love for you is like a stream of fresh water flowing into your cup. As you selflessly open your rim and allow the water to overflow down your sides, you water the flowers around you and they thrive and bless you back with a wonderful fragrance. But when you hoard your blessings it is like putting a lid on the rim of your cup. From then on, you have more than enough water for yourself but the freshness fades and your cup gets stale. In addition, you no longer bless those around you and before long, the environment of your life stinks! (much like the poverty stained spots on Earth)

It is far better to open our hearts and hands (and wallets) to our fellow man so that God can continually refresh our lives with more and more love and blessing to share. If we fail to share what God freely provides us, we risk losing everything in the long run. Matthew 21:43 shares this truth using the term "Kingdom of God" in place of "love and blessing".

> Therefore I tell you that the kingdom of God will be taken away from you and given to a people who will produce its fruit.

This verse comes from the parable of the tenants. It teaches the value of honorable stewardship as well as accepting God's son as His representative in your life. When we realize that what we have has been entrusted to us by God, and that we should be managing it according to his wishes, we realize (or make real) God's love in our lives. When that happens, we expand our family, make many friends and gain honor. And if we are ever found in need, those same friends can be there for us because we made it possible for them to do so by our generosity to them.

You'd be surprised how one kind thing you do today can be returned to you five or ten years down the road, when you need it the most. Believe it or not, this same principle applies at an international level as well. If we lift other countries and peoples up out of the mire, they may very well be the ones helping America down the road.

Change We Can Really Believe In

As I have said before, this country was absolutely founded on Judeo-Christian principles. Yes we have made mistakes, as have all other countries. We are still relatively young. We are learning. The question is, what are we learning and who are we learning from? If you look at our own wealth distribution here in America, it would appear that we are taught that greed is very good. The American dream somehow changed from a goal of life, liberty and the pursuit of happiness to capitalizing on the opportunity to become rich, even if it's at the expense of others; many others!

The distribution of wealth in America has never been so unbalanced. It isn't that we have 10% of our population working that much harder then the other 90%. The problem is a systemic, cultural adherence to the notion that it's acceptable to make as much money as you can get away with without worrying about who you're hurting to get it. There are numerous websites that share wealth distribution data. I found the following on *http://www.dailypaul.com:*

US wealth distribution:
10% of US citizens own 70.9% of all US assets.

Top 1% own 38.1%
Top 96-99% own 21.3%
Top 90-95% own 11.5%
Middle 41-89% own 28.9%

Bottom 40% of our population has 0.2% of all wealth!

Obviously, Capitalism without the will of God is rather detrimental to the US populace. If we applied the "cup in a flower bed" analogy it would appear that almost half the country is drying up from lack of blessing while the top 10% are swimming in wealth with the top 1% drowning in it. Am I saying that Socialism would fix this? Aaahhh…NO! Removing Capitalism and replacing it with Socialism would make matters worse. However, either platform of government guided by the will of God and the teachings of Jesus Christ would work much better for everyone involved. The rich can still be rich, the poor could be lifted out of poverty and the middle class could afford to get out and stay out of debt. Our country could then be in the position to lead the way for others.

I'll dare to take it one step further and say that if everyone in America who claims to be a Christian could get out of debt and afford to tithe; we could resolve many, if not all of the world's poverty related issues. All the children of the world could have clean water, proper medical care, a good education and adequate nutrition. What an unimaginable, unavoidable and super powerful witness that would be to the world. With results like that, no one could argue that Christianity works.

What we need is to allow God back into our lives. We need God back in our schools, back in our courts and back into the hearts of our government. I'm not saying we need to force people to believe. We couldn't do that if we tried. I'm saying we need to give them back both sides of the story instead of just the secular side. We need to allow Intelligent Design equal shelf and chalk board space in our universities as well as grades K through 12.. People need to hear the unselfish truth, not just the selfish, self centered version.

Have you ever really read the Constitution and understood exactly what it says regarding the idea of keeping the State and Church separate? This is the wording taken from the First Amendment to the United States Constitution:

> "Congress shall make no law respecting an establishment of religion, or prohibiting the free exercise thereof . . ."

So there you have it in what I feel is very understandable text. First; our government has no business creating or enforcing "official" prayers or practices of worship or favoring a denomination of Christianity or any other faith based belief system. Simply put; no laws to establish a government backed religion. All the Atheists can clap now! Or can they?

The second part goes on to say that the government can't prohibit the free exercise of prayer or worship either. So what does that mean? Since my premise is to bring God back into our lives, I will cut to the chase. If there is a consensus that implies; if it's a public school, paid for with tax dollars, then it's theoretically a government run school, (and teachers are theoretically government employees representing constitutional rules) then it means that if a football team wants to thank God out on the field, they have the Government given right to do so!

Teachers don't have the right to tell kids they must believe in Jesus or Allah or Evolution but they have the right and duty to share all theories of truth with children. That means that in the science room, children should be taught about Intelligent Design and theoretical purpose for life every bit as much as Evolution based on survival of the fittest.

If you use statistics as a factual truth gauge; the chances

that Darwin's theory of the origin of life is the way it really happened is about a gazillion to 1 against. (But don't believe me, check the facts and do the math yourself) The chances that our planet is positioned exactly the way it is, with its' precise orbit, axis, speed of movement, location in the galaxy and its' distance from the sun; every specification met to allow life to exist…***all by accident?*** That kind of denial reminds me of something my Mom taught me to say whenever I was asking for something…PLEASE!!!!!!

The way I see it, the pendulum has swung both ways. In the beginning, our country was established, organized and governed by Christians. The separation of church and state really stemmed from the issue of contrasting theologies; mainly between the Quakers, Congregationalists and those that followed the Church of England. Blind faith was accepted as good reason for the populace and much of what we now know in science was a mystery then. Now some two hundred years later, the pendulum swings to the other extreme which is to remove God from society and bow to the gods of detached science, political correctness and relativism. Maybe it's time someone with a functioning brain and all too human heart stand up and stop the pendulum in the middle so that we can have balance.

Who says we have to be fierce capitalists that judge value by quarterly earnings and black bottom lines? Who says we have to be liberal socialists who govern with the extended hands of entitlement? Why should good, hard working folks be so heavily taxed so the government can pay the poor just enough to stay needy while the rich grab more for themselves? Why can't we be a people who work hard, play hard and govern ourselves with humility, Godly justice, charity and compassion? We need, at every level, to stop living by what we can get away with and start living by what is right for mankind.

We can be the City on a Hill! Imagine what the words "Capitol Hill" would stand for if we all learned to love as Jesus loves. It would stand for a form of capitalism that is like a shining beacon of hope set on a high ground for the entire world to see. The key is in breaking the selfishness out of the American dream. We need to learn the value of life, liberty and the pursuit of happiness for humanity before we can really achieve it for ourselves with a clean conscience. To do that, we need to put God first, others second and ourselves last. It needs to be done at an individual level and it needs to be done yesterday!

I don't know what the future holds, or where our country and people will ultimately end up. Will we go down in history as a good people, or as a selfish people who lived to feel good? Will we perish like others before us; as a nation whose selfish corruption destroyed them, or will we allow God's influence to bring us up, and set us high on a lamp stand as a light to the world?

I pray that we go down in history as a nation that ultimately made a conscious decision to bless God by putting Him first, others second and ourselves last. The mathematical truth of it all is simply this; if America blesses God, then

God will continue to bless America. To achieve this; the very best scenario, we need to work together at every level, and learn to love the way God loves. This is truly our only real hope!

Thank You!

Thank you for reading this book. I hope it inspires you to reevaluate your purpose and the very real potential you have to make a difference in our world. I've met a lot of people throughout my life and most all of them have regrets of one kind or another. But I've never met anyone who regretted their relationship with Jesus Christ or the boundless love they gained and shared through it.

Of all the lessons life will teach us, there is no more important value then when we learn to love the way God wants us to. May you be blessed and highly favored in His sight for the love you give.

Sincerely, In Christ,
Dan Gilman

Index

All Bible references taken from The New International Version found online at ***http://www.biblegateway.com***

All definitions taken from the Merriam-Webster Online dictionary found at ***http://m-w.com/***

Cherokee Chief story…Author Unknown

Switchfoot: Are You Who You Want To Be; The Beautiful Letdown; Red Int/Red Ink Feb. 2003

Alexis de Tocqueville; The Greatness of America; as quoted by Dwight D. Eisenhower Nov. 1952 (unverified)

Heaven….Randy Alcorn; Tyndale House Publishers Oct. 2004

Mount Rushmore National Memorial Park History

National Park Service, U.S. Department of the Interior

Lee Strobel's "A Case for..." series; Zondervan 1998-2007

Pilgrims' Progress" by John Bunyan. DVD film put out by DRC Films, LLC in 2008.

Nicole Nordeman: Brave; Brave; Sparrow Records May 2005

"The Marketing of Evil", David Kupelian; WND Books Aug. 2005

Anxiety Disorders Association of America, "The Economic Burden of Anxiety Disorders," a study commissioned by ADAA and published in The Journal of Clinical Psychiatry, Vol. 60, No. 7, July 1999

Friedrich Nietzsche, Human, All Too Human, 1878

Robert Frost, The Road Not taken; Henry Holt and Company 1955

Louie Giglio: Indescribable; The Passion of the Heart; Passion Talk Series; Sparrow Records, Sixsteps Records 2005, 2009

Poverty information Data taken from Compassion International and Wikipedia Websites

Wealth Distribution; http://www.dailypaul.com/node/111232 posted 10/18/2009 in Daily Paul Liberty Forum

Breinigsville, PA USA
03 January 2011
252562BV00001B/1/P